When a Name Becomes a Game: Negotiating the Macedonian Identity

Victor Sinadinoski[1]

‖‖‖‖‖‖‖‖‖‖‖‖‖‖‖‖‖‖‖‖‖
I0411188

'The Macedonian' should by no means be regarded as a Bulgarian, Serb or Greek as 'he' is, on the first place, a political 'slave.' [2]

Our Macedonian grandfathers and fathers struggled and shed their blood for the liberty of the Greeks and the Serbs and for the liberation of Bulgaria; they did not spare for the common liberty of us all. Now the time has come for them to prove true descendants of their famous liberators and advocates and to help their fellows in the liberation of Macedonia from its five centuries of slavery. [3]

Chauvinism is poisoning the soul of humanity. We Macedonians hate no one and have no pretensions. We search in the darkness for a friend. [4]

My only reservation about the Macedonians is that we don't have more of them. [5]

No-one has a right to impose on a nation how to define itself ... no-one has a right to cut off a nation's national, linguistic and cultural roots. [6]

---

[1] University of Michigan, B.S. 2007; Vermont Law School, J.D. and M.E.L.P Candidate 2012.
[2] Marinov, Tchavdar, *We, the Macedonians: The Paths of Macedonian Supra-Nationalism (1878-1912)*, in *We, the People: Politics of National Peculiarity in Southeastern Europe* by Diana Mishkova, 122 (2009).
[3] *Rules of the Macedonian Rebel Committee*, Rule 194
http://documents-mk.blogspot.com/2009/12/blog-post_30.html . Last accessed February 27, 2011.
[4] Kaplan, Robert D., *Balkan Ghosts: A Journey Throughout History*, 60 (1993). Quote by Orde Ivanovski.
[5] McNamara, Sally and Morgan L. Roach, *The Obama Administration Must Push for Macedonia's Accession to NATO at the Lisbon Summit*, The Heritage Foundation. Web Memo No. 3037, 2 (2010). Quote by US Lieutenant Colonel Joseph Gleichenhaus.
[6] Vangelov, Ognen, *The Greek Veto the Macedonian Identity*, 4.

Table of Contents

Introduction

Greece's dispute with the Republic of Macedonia (Macedonia) over the latter's name is not solely, nor primarily, about a name. Rather, Greece's quarrel is the most recent chapter in a tale of constant struggles for identity, land, and resources, fused with episodes of feverish nationalism, hostile political maneuvering and suspicious foreign interests. This current clash between the two southern Balkan countries is rooted in ancient Macedonia's conquest of the ancient Greek states, and spans several centuries of relative obscurity until the arrival of the brutal Ottomans. Macedonia's struggles to free herself from 500 years of Ottoman rule, along with aspirations of her neighbors to conquer and annihilate the Macedonian identity, rechristened this millennia-old contention and captured the heart of European diplomacy. The Great Powers and Macedonia's neighbors endeavored to bury the Macedonian dispute in the early 1900s by splitting Macedonia into several pieces, with each neighbor annexing an organ. Throughout the 20th century, certain Balkan nations assimilated, exiled and murdered Macedonians to fulfill an ethnic cleansing campaign of the Macedonians. Hence, today's relatively peaceful name dispute, despite its twenty-year old history, is only a snapshot of the overarching Macedonian Question, also known as the Macedonian Problem or the Macedonian Syndrome.

Regardless of how historians and politicians have phrased it, the Macedonian Question has implanted two centuries of violence and bloodshed in the Balkans, and has left the ethnic Macedonians destitute and sentenced to nonexistence. Yet, the Macedonians survive and persevere with their struggles, to the public and silent dismay of many. Thus, the situation remains "as alive and problematic as ever."[7] Unfortunately, "[h]ardly any other country in Europe is probably regarded by its neighbors as much [as] of an imposition as the Republic of Macedonia."[8] Macedonia's neighbors have ignored international legal obstacles and glorified hate-based ideologies in their quests to obtain Macedonian territory and eradicate the Macedonian identity, language, state and people. Justifiably, Macedonians want to erase this question mark plastered onto their identity.

This paper discusses the history, politics and legality of Macedonia's ongoing saga with Greece over Macedonia's name. The structure of this paper is as follows. In Part A, I first explore the history of Macedonia, from ancient times until the present day. Then I dive into a recount of Macedonia's struggle for freedom from the Ottoman Empire and the following years that resulted in Macedonia's division. Next, I investigate Macedonia and the Macedonians after the early 20th century Balkan wars until the People's Republic of Macedonia declared independence from Yugoslavia as the Republic of Macedonia in the 1990s. Finally, I analyze the dispute with Greece with a chronological approach, while also injecting major events that have directly and indirectly affected the name dispute.

In Part B, I consider several major reasons why discussions and negotiations have not resulted in any meaningful solutions. These reasons include, but are not limited to, Greece's denial of the existence of a Macedonian ethnic identity; an obsession with the glories and successes of ancient-Macedonia; foreign influence in the forms of national governments and ethnic Diasporas; internal political struggles and divisions that have plagued both Greece and Macedonia; a highly adversarial Greek tone and position; and Greece's general lack of reasonableness regarding the name 'Macedonia'.

---

[7] Poulton, Hugh, *The Balkans: Minorities and States in Conflict*, 55 (1994).

[8] Wieland, Carsten, *One Macedonia with Three Faces: Domestic Debates and Nation Concept*, 1.

Finally, in Part C, I outline some solutions to the dispute, if a solution is even possible. First, I list reasons for why a peaceful solution through negotiations and discussions is a better choice than any other option. Second, I then consider some solutions that can be found through negotiations and discussion. Finally, I highlight the likely alternatives to negotiations, which include the status quo and the force of international court decisions.

The Macedonian-Greek name dispute is a dispute which involves much more than just the name of a country. Consequently, any solution to the dispute will involve much more than discussions about a name – it will involve an acknowledgment of historical and present wrongdoings; it will involve a willingness to embrace collaboration; and it will involve the principles of peace, justice and freedom. Hopefully, Macedonia and Greece can overcome this rift and set an example that the future people of this world can look back to with respect and admiration. If not, the dreadful past that has continuously plagued the Balkans may be only one bullet away from being reignited.

Critical Terminology

* *Ethnic Macedonian* and *Macedonian* refer to a person who embraces a Macedonian identity and culture as separate from any other culture or identity, especially as distinct from a Slav, Greek, Bulgarian or Serb identity.
* *Macedonian citizen* refers to a person who is a citizen of the Republic of Macedonia and is not necessarily an ethnic Macedonian.
* *Skopjian*, *Slav-Macedonian* and *Fyromian* are degrading terms used by some people to describe the Macedonians.
* *Ethnic Greek* and *Greek* refer to a person who embraces the Greek identity and culture as separate from any other culture or identity.
* *Greek citizen* refers to a person who is a citizen of Greece and is not necessarily an ethnic Greek.
* *Republic of Macedonia* and *Macedonia* refers to the constitutional name of the country recognized in the United Nations as the 'former Yugoslav Republic of Macedonia' and in over 130 countries as the Republic of Macedonia. Macedonia is bordered by Serbia[9] to the north, Bulgaria to the east, Greece to the south, and Albania to the west.
* *Geographic Macedonia* is the ethnic Macedonians' homeland, which includes the Republic of Macedonia (also known as Vardar Macedonia), Aegean Macedonia (currently occupied by Greece), Pirin Macedonia (currently occupied by Bulgaria), and a tiny segment within Albania's borders (Mala Prespa and Golo Brdo). Aegean Macedonian constitutes over 51% of geographic Macedonia; Pirin Macedonia constitutes 10% of geographic Macedonia; the Republic of Macedonia constitutes about 37% of geographic Macedonia; and Mala Prespa and Golo Brdo constitute just under 2% of geographic Macedonia.
* *Ancient Macedonia* refers to the time period that begins with the birth of the Macedonian kingdom and ends after the Roman occupation of Macedonia.

---

[9] As of this writing, the Serbian province of Kosovo is still not recognized by the United Nations as an independent country. Kosovo borders Macedonia to the northwest.

A. History

The Macedonian question may be summed up in the story of Mr. Omerić, which was told [to] me by Adam Wandruszka. Omerić, who was so called under the Jugoslav monarchy, became Omerov during the Bulgarian occupation in the Second World War and then Omerski for the Republic of Macedonia, which is part of the Jugoslav federation. His original name, Omer, was Turkish.[10]

1. From ancient Macedonia until the Ottoman arrival

Macedonia germinated over 3,000 years ago on the Balkan Peninsula. Over the course of several centuries, numerous tribes merged together to form ancient Macedonia.[11] This gradual formation took "the intermingling, amalgamation, and assimilation of various ethnic elements," out of which sprouted the first Macedonians.[12] Macedonia remained disjointed until the Argeadan Dynasty unified the Macedonians in the 7th century B.C.[13] A century later Macedonia became a Persian tributary, but only for a few decades.[14]

Throughout this early period, Macedonia hardly partook in the intellectual, social, and cultural progress of Greece;[15] and thus they did not regard themselves as Greeks.[16] It was not until Alexander I, around 440 BC, when Macedonia began to adopt certain elements of Greek culture as a deliberate policy[17] to Hellenize the Macedonian court and elite.[18] Macedonia further took advantage of opportunities to "enhance the court's power and the state's unity" after the Peloponnesian Wars in Greece (which did not involve Macedonia) during the second half of the 5th century B.C.[19]

Macedonia's "most glorious era" came to fruition when King Philip acquired the throne.[20] "Philip was a typical Macedonian nobleman – fiery in temperament, excessive in drink, and exceedingly fond of war, horses, beautiful women, and handsome young boys."[21] Almost immediately, in 359 B.C., Philip began subjugating the Greek states under Macedonian rule.[22] He even expelled and exiled Greek settlers, including Aristotle, who had settled Macedonia's coastline.[23] Phillip eventually conquered all of Greece in 338 B.C.[24] But he accomplished much more for Macedonia than simply conquering Greece:

---

[10] Magris, Claudio, *Danube*, 348 (1989).
[11] Underdown, Michael, *Background to the Macedonian Question*, 2 (1994).
[12] Rossos, Andrew, *Macedonia and the Macedonians*, 11 (2008).
[13] Underdown, Michael, *Background to the Macedonian Question*, 2 (1994).
[14] *Id.*
[15] Floudas, Demetrius A., *Pardon? A Conflict for a Name?: Fyrom's Dispute with Greece Revisited*, 1.
[16] Underdown, Michael, *Background to the Macedonian Question*, 2 (1994).
[17] *Id.*
[18] Rossos, Andrew, *Macedonia and the Macedonians*, 13 (2008).
[19] *Id.*
[20] *Id.* at 14.
[21] Freeman, Philip, *Alexander the Great*, 9 (2011).
[22] Underdown, Michael, *Background to the Macedonian Question*, 2 (1994).
[23] *The Macedonian-Greek Conflict: The Age Long Conflict between the Greeks and the Macedonians*, http://www.historyofmacedonia.org/MacedonianGreekConflict/conflict.html
[24] Underdown, Michael, *Background to the Macedonian Question*, 2 (1994).

He transformed the country from a weak and fragmented land to Balkan dominance. He weakened the clan aristocracy and centralized administration. His financial reforms, including introduction of a gold coin, spurred growth of trade and commerce and made Macedonia a political and economic factor in the eastern Mediterranean. He reorganized the army; modernized its training, tactics, and weaponry; and harnessed it for territorial expansion.[25]

After Phillip was assassinated, his son (eventually to be known as Alexander the Great) became heir to the throne. Alexander extended his father's kingdom eastward, and after defeating the Persians, he "proclaimed himself successor of the Persian 'King of Kings'" and continued steering his troops into Central Asia.[26] His empire included vast stretches from the Balkans to India, and also consisted of Egypt, Libya and Cyrenaica to the south of Macedonia and Greece.[27]

Upon Alexander's death (the cause is still debated) the empire began to crumble,[28] especially because Alexander left no legitimate successor to the throne,[29] and because his empire was ungovernable.[30] The second Macedonian War at the beginning of the 2nd century B.C. witnessed the Romans invading the Balkans to support the growing anti-Macedonian coalition of the Greeks and eventually resulted in Macedonia's recognition of an independent Greece.[31] Perseus became the last Macedonian king and was defeated by the Romans in 168 BC.[32] Upon seizing control of Macedonia, the Romans divided Macedonia into four regions; and in 148 B.C., the Romans joined Epirus to Macedonia.[33] This new Roman province was now "a center for the [Roman] empire to project its strategic interests in the eastern Mediterranean."[34] When the Roman Empire was divided in 395 AD, Macedonia became part of the Byzantine Empire.[35] Eventually, Macedonia was invaded by Goths and Huns, and then by the Slavs in the 6th Century AD,[36] who decided to permanently settle in Macedonia.[37]

These Slavs probably originated in a geographic region shared by Poland, Ukraine, and Belarus.[38] When these Slavs came to Macedonia, they "absorbed the native inhabitants"[39] – Macedonia was not void of people during the Slavic migration. However, unlike their neighbors, the hybrid of Slavs and ancient Macedonians "did not form a medieval dynastic or territorial state carrying their name."[40] This resulted in several hardships for the Macedonians, especially politically and economically, as they could not

---

[25] Rossos, Andrew, *Macedonia and the Macedonians*, 14 (2008).
[26] *Id*. at 15.
[27] *Id*.
[28] Underdown, Michael, *Background to the Macedonian Question*, 3 (1994).
[29] Vangeli, Anastas, *Antiquity Musing: Reflections on the Greco-Macedonian Symbolic Contest over the Narratives of the Ancient Past*, 5 (2009).
[30] Rossos, Andrew, *Macedonia and the Macedonians*, 15 (2008).
[31] *Id*. at 16.
[32] Underdown, Michael, *Background to the Macedonian Question*, 3 (1994).
[33] *Id*.
[34] Rossos, Andrew, *Macedonia and the Macedonians*, 17 (2008).
[35] Underdown, Michael, *Background to the Macedonian Question*, 3 (1994).
[36] *Id*.
[37] Rossos, Andrew, *Macedonia and the Macedonians*, 18 (2008).
[38] *Id*. at 23.
[39] Id at 24.
[40] *Id*. at 19.

gain legitimacy from different empires and kingdoms that ruled their lands. Still, two saints of Macedonia, brothers Cyril and Methodius from Salonica,[41] played a central role during this period in inventing and developing the Cyrillic alphabet, which Orthodox Slavs still use today.[42]

In the 9th Centruy AD, Czar Samuil formed a Macedonian Kingdom "different from the former kingdom of the Bulgars…[i]n composition and character[…]"[43] For political reasons, though, Czar Samuil and the Byzantines regarded this Macedonian Kingdom as part of the Bulgarian empire.[44] This did not imply, however, any sort of ethnic or national Bulgarian element of the kingdom.[45] Czar Samuil eventually established the archbishopric in what is today known as the town of Ohrid, Macedonia.[46]

The Byzantine Empire regained Macedonia in the 11th century,[47] and Macedonians soon began embracing and accepting Christianity.[48] Macedonia eventually became known in Europe as "a major religious and cultural center."[49] Throughout the next centuries, as part of the Byzantine Empire, "the Macedonians fought foreign invaders, adventurers, and bandits who failed to dominate their land."[50] Michael Psellus of the 11th century explains an attempt by the Macedonians to stage a revolution:

> [T]he Macedonians thought that here at last was the oft-sought chance of revolution, and after a brief consultation between their leaders – they had long ago determined their aims – they stirred Tornicius to make his absurd attempt and encouraged themselves to give mutual undertakings to strike the daring blow. They got him out of the city by night, secretly, with the help of a few confederates – quite insignificant persons – and drove straight for Macedonia. […] So, pressing on without respite, they crossed the Macedonian border, seized Hadrian's city as an acropolis, and at once set to work.[51]

These struggles continued throughout the following centuries. Serbia eventually conquered Macedonia briefly in the 14th century until the Ottoman Empire took control, dominating Macedonia and the Balkan region until the twentieth century.[52]

2. Life under the Ottoman Empire

The Ottomans controlled most of Macedonia by the year 1400 A.D. and conquered it in its entirety by 1430.[53] For much of this time, life for the Macedonian peasants was

---

[41] *The Macedonian-Greek Conflict: The Age Long Conflict between the Greeks and the Macedonians*, http://www.historyofmacedonia.org/MacedonianGreekConflict/conflict.html
[42] Rossos, Andrew, *Macedonia and the Macedonians*, 33 (2008).
[43] *Id.*at 20.
[44] *Id.*
[45] *Id*. at 30.
[46] *Id.*
[47] Underdown, Michael, *Background to the Macedonian Question*, 3 (1994).
[48] Rossos, Andrew, *Macedonia and the Macedonians*, 24 (2008).
[49] *Id*. at 32.
[50] *The Macedonian-Greek Conflict: The Age Long Conflict between the Greeks and the Macedonians*, http://www.historyofmacedonia.org/MacedonianGreekConflict/conflict.html
[51] *Michael Psellus: Fourteen Byzantine Rulers*, 208 (1966).
[52] Underdown, Michael, *Background to the Macedonian Question*, 3 (1994).
[53] Rossos, Andrew, *Macedonia and the Macedonians*, 40 (2008).

neither good nor horrible. Although the Muslim Ottomans regarded the Macedonians as their inferiors, the Macedonians were "more secure than their ancestors had been under rapacious, native, landed aristocrats[.]"[54]

In the 16th and 17th centuries, ethnic Macedonians began forming adjuts, which were bands of a few dozen to a few hundred peasants who "attacked and robbed the estates and properties of Ottoman lords and ambushed tax collectors and trade caravans ... [and] rich Christian oligarchs and wealthy monasteries" in the summer months.[55] These adjuts were admired and protected by Macedonian Christians, and were further "romanticized ... in their folk songs, tales, and traditions as fighters against foreign exploitation and for social justice."[56] In 1689, one adjut's leader, Karpos, ignited a revolt which was initially successful for some weeks; however, the Ottomans eventually defeated him and squashed the rebellion.[57]

When the Ottoman Empire began to crumble in the 19th century, surrounding Balkan states took an interest in Macedonia.[58] Essentially, the annexation of Macedonia became a national interest of Greece, Serbia, and Bulgaria.[59] The reasons for pursuing Macedonia were mainly strategic and economic, particularly because Macedonia was a main route from the Mediterranean to central Europe, and because Macedonia contained an abundance of fertile land.[60] "[W]hoever would acquire Macedonia would dominate the Balkans."[61]

In 1870, the Bulgarian Exarchate wanted to create a distinct Bulgarian national identity for the Macedonian[62] speaking people of the region.[63] They initiated this campaign by founding schools and creating propaganda targeted at the Macedonian peasants.[64] This alarmed the Serbs and Greeks, who in turn commenced a similar crusade.[65] Macedonia's neighbors began the race to convert and assimilate her people.

As a result of the 1877-1878 Russo-Turkish war,[66] the Treaty of San Stefano was signed in 1878, and most of Macedonia was given to Bulgaria.[67] "The Russians, as patrons of the Bulgarians, [had] pressed for the inclusion of Macedonia under Bulgarian rule[.]"[68] But this was short-lived and the Powers of the time returned Macedonia to the Ottoman Empire within a few months.[69,70]

---

[54] *Id.* at 46.

[55] Id. at 53-54.

[56] *Id.* at 54.

[57] *Id.*

[58] Floudas, Demetrius A., *Pardon? A Conflict for a Name?: Fyrom's Dispute with Greece Revisited*, 2.

[59] *Id.*

[60] Rossos, Andrew, *Macedonia and the Macedonians*, 73 (2008).

[61] *Id.*

[62] In Floudas' article, he used the word "Slav" instead of Macedonian. I believe the evidence exists that this language being spoken was the Macedonian language.

[63] Floudas, Demetrius A., *Pardon? A Conflict for a Name?: Fyrom's Dispute with Greece Revisited*, 2.

[64] *Id.*

[65] *Id.*

[66] Apostolov, Mico, *The Macedonian Question -- Changes in Content Over Time*, iii (2006).

[67] Underdown, Michael, *Background to the Macedonian Question*, 3 (1994).

[68] Weiner, Myron, *The Macedonian Syndrome: An Historical Model of International Relations and Political Development*, 23 World Politics 4, 671 (1971).

[69] Apostolov, Mico, *The Macedonian Question -- Changes in Content Over Time*, iii (2006).

[70] *The Macedonian-Greek Conflict: The Age Long Conflict between the Greeks and the Macedonians*, http://www.historyofmacedonia.org/MacedonianGreekConflict/conflict.html

After the Conference of Berlin in 1878, the Macedonians experienced unfathomable horrors, as Jasminka Udovicki highlights:

> ...Macedonia was again plunged into despair. Unchecked by foreign powers, Turkey levied excessive taxes on the exhausted population. Those unable to pay were locked up, beaten, and tortured. Wanton violence descended on the land. Captured men had their eyes gouged and ears cut off. Women and girls were raped. Never having known the good life, Macedonians accepted their brutal history, and poverty, with fatalism of the doomed.[71]

As a result of these injustices, several courageous Macedonians formed the Macedonian Rebel Committee. Included among the 211 aims and rules of the committee was: the desire to extend the uprising throughout all of Macedonia; a proclamation that people who feel themselves Macedonians and who "love the freedom of their fatherland" were participating in the uprising; and to allow all people, "regardless of faith and nationality," to participate in this freedom movement as long as they loved freedom.[72] Referring to the patriotic duties of all Macedonians, the Macedonian Rebel Committee demonstrated how this was a national and political movement.[73]

Macedonians then attempted a major rebellion in 1881, but were swiftly defeated by the Turks "with extraordinary brutality."[74] Once again, in the mid-1880s, Bulgaria's Macedonian refugees, who had been increasing steadily, seized weapons from a Bulgarian arsenal and formed two armed bands that crossed back into Macedonia to maintain the Macedonian combat.[75] The Macedonians in Bulgaria resorted to such measures because, unfortunately, the Bulgarian governments throughout the 1880s did not support the Macedonian nationalist movements.[76] Still, the Macedonian nationalist movement only gained more momentum as a consequence:

> [T]he anonymous article "An Opinion Concerning the Resolution of Macedonian Question" published in 1889 in the newspaper Makedonija [Macedonia], edited by [...] Macedonian activist Kosta Šahov [...] promotes the idea of an independent struggle of the entire population of the region against Ottoman domination. For this task, [the author] recommends the usage of the common denominator 'Macedonians' [makedonci] for all the ethnic and confessional communities of the region. 'We, the Macedonians' [nie makedoncite], stresses the anonymous activist, should not desire any unification with a neighbor state whatsoever, as the other neighbors would also try to get their share and Macedonia would be torn up. Regardless of their 'nationality' [narodnost]–be they 'Bulgarians, Turks, Vlachs, etc.'–all Macedonians have 'the same interests' and should work for the 'political liberty' of their 'land.'[77]

---

[71] Udovicki, Jasminka, *The Bonds and Fault Lines*, in *Burn This House: The Making and Unmaking of Yugoslavia*, 33 (1997).

[72] *Rules of the Macedonian Rebel Committee*,
http://documents-mk.blogspot.com/2009/12/blog-post_30.html . Last accessed February 27, 2011.

[73] *Id*. Rule 79 states in part that "A patriotic duty of every Macedonian is to inform the ... Macedonian Army immediately of anything he has found out about the enemy..."

[74] Udovicki, Jasminka, *The Bonds and Fault Lines*, in *Burn This House: The Making and Unmaking of Yugoslavia*, 33 (1997).

[75] Pelt, Mogens, *Organized Violence in the Service of Nation Building*, in *Ottomans into Europeans: State and Institution Building in South Eastern Europe*, 235 (2010).

[76] Gledhill, John and Charles King, *Institutions, Violence, and Captive States in Balkan History*, in *Ottomans into Europeans: State and Institution Building in South Eastern Europe*, 256 (2010).

[77] Marinov, Tchavdar, *We, the Macedonians: The Paths of Macedonian Supra-Nationalism (1878-1912)*, in *We, the People: Politics of National Peculiarity in Southeastern Europe* by Diana Mishkova, 113 (2009).

In the meantime, the campaigns to assert control over Macedonia progressed. In 1885, the Serbians began claiming that the people of Macedonia were Serbs, and Greece declared its wish to free all Greeks in the Balkans, starting with Macedonia.[78] The Serbs even signed a treaty with the Austria-Hungary Empire in the beginning of 1889 that gave Austria's blessing for Serbia to annex lands south of Serbia, such as Vardar Macedonia, "as far as the circumstances [would] permit."[79] The Serbs were planning to take over Macedonia while Bulgaria's Prime Minister Stefan Stambolov began working with the Ottomans in 1887 to repress the Macedonian national movement and keep Macedonia within the Ottoman Empire.[80]

The main Macedonian nationalist movement, the Internal Macedonian Revolutionary Organization (IMRO), formed on October 23, 1893 by six people[81] in Stip, Macedonia.[82] The organization was split between those who wanted to unite Macedonia under Bulgarian rule and those who wanted to establish an independent state that would incorporate all Macedonian regions -- Vardar Macedonia, Pirin Macedonia and Aegean Macedonia.[83],[84] The latter element intended to free the Macedonians "from the devastating foreign—Bulgarian, Greek, Serbian—propaganda, intervention, and terror, which split the Slav Macedonians in family, village, town, and homeland into antagonistic 'parties,' or camps, and threatened annexation or partition."[85] "Macedonians were to free their land for the Macedonians."[86]

These courageous men were "led by the young schoolteacher Goce Delcev,"[87] "a wise and broadminded insurgent leader [who] called for the elimination of chauvinist propaganda and nationalist dissention that divided and weakened the population of Macedonia[.]"[88] In 1894, Petâr Poparsov, also a Macedonian revolutionary, "edited ... a brochure where he expressed quite a sharp criticism towards the 'authoritarian' and 'corrupted' course of action of the Bulgarian Church[,]" or also known as the Bulgarian Exarchate.[89] The Bulgarian Exarchate "opposed the revolutionary agenda of the organization [... and] considered that revolutionaries would only complicate the political status quo and hinder the formation of a powerful Bulgarian intelligentsia in Macedonia."[90] Actually, one of the first armed conflicts that the IMRO participated in was against pro-Bulgarian Exarchate followers.[91] It was apparent that a definite split existed

---

[78] Poulton, Hugh, *The Balkans: Minorities and States in Conflict*, 47 (1994).

[79] Grosek, Edward, *The Secret Treaties of History*, 132 (2004).

[80] Gledhill, John and Charles King, *Institutions, Violence, and Captive States in Balkan History*, in *Ottomans into Europeans: State and Institution Building in South Eastern Europe*, 256 (2010).

[81] Apostolov, Mico, *The Macedonian Question -- Changes in Content Over Time*, iii (2006).

[82] Kaplan, Robert D., *Balkan Ghosts: A Journey Throughout History*, 56 (1993).

[83] Underdown, Michael, *Background to the Macedonian Question*, 3 (1994).

[84] Poulton, Hugh, *The Balkans: Minorities and States in Conflict*, 48 (1994).

[85] Rossos, Andrew, *Macedonia and the Macedonians*, 103 (2008).

[86] *Id.*

[87] Udovicki, Jasminka, *The Bonds and Fault Lines*, in *Burn This House: The Making and Unmaking of Yugoslavia*, 33 (1997).

[88] *Id.*

[89] Marinov, Tchavdar, *We, the Macedonians: The Paths of Macedonian Supra-Nationalism (1878-1912)*, in *We, the People: Politics of National Peculiarity in Southeastern Europe* by Diana Mishkova, 115 (2009).

[90] *Id.*

[91] *Id.*

between the Macedonian political loyalty and the Bulgarian national loyalty by 1895.[92]

Before the dawn of the new century, Macedonians formed an anarchist committee in Geneva, Switzerland.[93] These ambitious Macedonians strived for an independent Macedonia and a Macedonia for all Macedonians.[94] They worked in opposition to "Bulgarian chauvinism" and the idea of uniting Macedonia with Bulgaria, and also against "Greek and Serbian ambitions."[95] By 1902, Bulgarians were afraid that these and other Macedonians would be successful, so they "sought to provoke reprisals by the Turks against Macedonian villages in order to facilitate eventual Bulgarian intervention."[96]

The Macedonians, Greeks, Bulgarians and Serbians continued forming armed groups, and fought each other, as well as the Ottomans, in Macedonia from 1903-1910.[97] The Macedonians boasted 30,000 fighters,[98] thanks to the efforts of the IMRO, but faced a reinforced 300,000-strong Turkish army.[99] Still, on August 2, 1903, Macedonians staged an uprising and formed the first republic in the Balkans, the Krushevo Republic,[100] which became a "democratic commune"[101] with Nikola Karev as its first elected president.[102] The republic did not last and the uprising did not succeed, falling in two months, mostly because not one nation decided to support the Macedonians – not Russia, not Great Britain, not Serbia, not Greece.[103] Writing in 1913 about why France did not come to Macedonia's aid with their struggles against the Ottoman oppressors, Stephen Duggan stated:

> Moreover France has millions invested in the Balkan peninsula, and her foreign policy is, to a great extent, dominated by her desire to protect the savings of her peasants invested abroad. She wants peace at almost any price; and, while desirous of seeing conditions improved in Macedonia, she was unwilling to participate in violent measures which might disturb the status quo in the Balkans and bring on a European war.[104]

In other words, an oppressed Macedonian nation was more beneficial to France than a free Macedonian nation. However, even though no consolidation, the uprising did make Macedonia a primary discussion of European diplomacy at the time,[105] all while "[t]he Turks took terrible revenge [on the Macedonians], slaughtering whole villages."[106] Many Macedonians had no choice but to flee to Bulgaria, Serbia and the United States.[107]

In 1909, Bulgaria and Serbia came to another agreement, stating in part that if Macedonia could not achieve autonomy, Bulgaria and Serbia would partition

---

[92] *Id.* at 116.

[93] *Id.* at 123.

[94] *Id.*

[95] *Id.*

[96] Shea, John, *Macedonia and Greece: The Struggle to Define a New Nation*, 169.

[97] Floudas, Demetrius A., *Pardon? A Conflict for a Name?: Fyrom's Dispute with Greece Revisited*, 2.

[98] Shea, John, *Macedonia and Greece: The Struggle to Define a New Nation*, 169.

[99] *Id.*

[100] Apostolov, Mico, *The Macedonian Question -- Changes in Content Over Time*, iv (2006).

[101] Shea, John, *Macedonia and Greece: The Struggle to Define a New Nation*, 169.

[102] *Id.* at. 171

[103] *Id.* at 169.

[104] Duggan, Stephen P., European Diplomacy and the Balkan Problem. 28(1): Mar. 1913. Pg. 99.

[105] Apostolov, Mico, *The Macedonian Question -- Changes in Content Over Time*, iv (2006).

[106] Shea, John, *Macedonia and Greece: The Struggle to Define a New Nation*, 169.

[107] *Id.* at 170.

Macedonia.[108] This actually happened when the Ottomans retreated from Macedonia[109] only shortly after "Bulgaria and Serbia concluded a pact that provided for the division of Macedonia between them" in 1912.[110] This was very disappointing to the Macedonians, because, as they were "[u]nable to free themselves from the Ottoman yoke [and] welcomed the Greek, Serbian and Bulgarian armies in 1912 as their liberators[,] […] instead of being liberated they quickly found themselves occupied and their state partitioned."[111] The love triangle between Bulgaria, Serbia and Greece quickly became confusing when, in the next month, Bulgaria and Greece signed a Treaty of Alliance and Defense.[112] Serbia then signed four treaties with Greece in 1913 detailing the areas they both wished to annex from Bulgaria.[113] Expectedly, the harmony and peace did not last long as Bulgaria strived for more land than it had bargained for, and thus attacked Greece and Serbia in 1913.[114]

Regardless of the alliances, the wars amounted to mass ethnic cleansing of Macedonians. In 1913 alone, over 160 Macedonian villages were burned to the ground.[115] Further, the Greeks burned 4,000 houses in the city of Serres, along with rounding up hundreds of Macedonians and executing them.[116]

Meanwhile, in St. Petersburg, Russia, the Macedonians were pleading not to be divided by her neighbors.[117] These Macedonians stated that Macedonia had the natural and historical rights to self-determination; that they "organized innumerable insurrections and distinguished themselves by determination and courage" to fight for this self-determination; that over 6,000 Macedonian soldiers defeated the Turks in Kumanovo (a town in Macedonia) as Serbian fighters retreated; that the Serbs and Bulgarians remain silent about such Macedonian victories and do not let anyone speak about them; that Macedonia belongs to the Macedonians; and that "the partition of Macedonia by its brothers is the most unjust act in the history of peoples, a violation of the rights of Man, a disgrace to the whole Slav race."[118]

Yet, these two Balkan wars eventually led to the Treaty of Bucharest on August 10th, 1913,[119] which resulted in Macedonia's division, where Greece annexed over 50% of geographic Macedonia, Bulgaria 10%, and Serbia about 40%. [120] A small part of geographic Macedonia eventually went to Albania.[121] For the first time in history, a

---

[108] Apostolov, Mico, *The Macedonian Question -- Changes in Content Over Time*, v (2006).
[109] *Id.*
[110] Willmott, H.P., *World War I*, 22 (2009).
[111] Stefov, Risto, *Greek-Macedonian Name Dispute*.
http://maknews.com/html/articles/stefov/Greek-MacedonianNameDisputeSimplefied.html . (2007).
[112] *Treaty of Alliance and Defense Between Bulgaria and Greece*,
http://www.pollitecon.com/html/treaties/Treaty_Of_Alliance_And_Defense_Between_Bulgaria_And_Greece.html .
[113] Grosek, Edward, *The Secret Treaties of History*, 149-50 (2004).
[114] Apostolov, Mico, *The Macedonian Question -- Changes in Content Over Time*, v (2006).
[115] Medichkov, Peter, *Greek Acts Against the Macedonians: 1912-1994*,
http://maknews.com/html/articles/medichkov/medichkov_report.htm .
[116] *The Macedonian-Greek Conflict: The Age Long Conflict between the Greeks and the Macedonians*,
http://www.historyofmacedonia.org/MacedonianGreekConflict/conflict.html
[117] Seraphinoff, Michael, *Dimensions of the Greek-Macedonian Name Dispute*, 4 (2008).
[118] *Id.* at 4-6.
[119] Medichkov, Peter, *Greek Acts Against the Macedonians: 1912-1994*,
http://maknews.com/html/articles/medichkov/medichkov_report.htm .
[120] Floudas, Demetrius A., *Pardon? A Conflict for a Name?: Fyrom's Dispute with Greece Revisited*, 2.
[121] Human Rights Watch, *Denying Ethnic Identity: The Macedonians in Greece*, 4 (1994).

segment of Macedonia became administered under Greece.[122] This is basically how Macedonia remains divided today.[123]

3. From Macedonia's division to the emergence of the Republic of Macedonia

Two-thirds of Macedonia is under foreign occupation and still to be liberated.[124]

Between 1913 and 1926 ethnic Macedonians constituted the largest ethnic group in Aegean Macedonia. [125] However, this quickly changed with the large population movements of Macedonians leaving Aegean Macedonia for Bulgaria, and Greeks leaving Vardar Macedonia for Greece.[126] After Macedonia's division and before the majority of these population exchanges and forced exiles, the assassination of the Austrian Archduke in Sarajevo in 1914 sparked World War I. This war brought to the Balkans and Macedonia much more bloodshed. For example, throughout the war, Bulgaria had its sights on annexing Vardar Macedonia from Serbia. [127] As one author put it, Bulgaria's "heart's desire" was to annex this part of Macedonia.[128] On October 21, 1915, Bulgarian troops invaded Skopje and fought French soldiers.[129] Eventually, Bulgaria was forced out of Vardar Macedonia.

The population exchanges mentioned before were ultimately anchored in a 1919 Greek-Bulgarian Convention,[130] known as the Convention of Neuilly, which called for the migration of ethnic Macedonians from Greece to Bulgaria and "the liquidation of their properties."[131] The Treaty of Versailles was signed in the same year, as was the ratification and endorsement of the 1913 Bucharest Treaty by England and France.[132] The 1920 Treaty of Serves was then passed to protect Greece's Macedonian minority and to allow use of the Macedonian language in education and for official purposes. [133]

The Treaty of Lausanne in 1923 produced exchanges of hundreds of thousands of Greeks in Turkey with hundreds of thousands of Turks in Aegean Macedonia. Furthermore, most ethnic Macedonians in the border zones and near railway lines were deported to Thessaly and the Greek Islands, as Greece became afraid these Macedonians would collaborate with Turkey in the event of a war.[134] Moreover, the families of ethnic

---

[122] Floudas, Demetrius A., *Pardon? A Conflict for a Name?: Fyrom's Dispute with Greece Revisited*, 6.
[123] Underdown, Michael, *Background to the Macedonian Question*, 4 (1994).
[124] Kaplan, Robert D., *Balkan Ghosts: A Journey Throughout History*, 66-67 (1993). Quoate by Ante Popovski.
[125] Human Rights Watch, *Denying Ethnic Identity: The Macedonians in Greece*, 5 (1994).
[126] Underdown, Michael, *Background to the Macedonian Question*, 4 (1994).
[127] Gilbert, Martin, *The First World War: A Complete History*, 205 (1994).
[128] Strachan, Hew, *The First World War*, 156 (2003).
[129] Gilbert, Martin, *The First World War: A Complete History*, 205 (1994).
[130] Underdown, Michael, *Background to the Macedonian Question*, 4 (1994).
[131] Kontogiorgi, Elisabeth, *Population Exchange in Greek Macedonia : The Forced Settlement of Refugees, 1922-1930*, 201 (2006).
[132] Medichkov, Peter, *Greek Acts Against the Macedonians: 1912-1994*, http://maknews.com/html/articles/medichkov/medichkov_report.htm .
[133] Underdown, Michael, *Background to the Macedonian Question*, 4 (1994).
[134] Kontogiorgi, Elisabeth, *Population Exchange in Greek Macedonia : The Forced Settlement of Refugees, 1922-1930*, 206-7 (2006).

Macedonian men who did not either serve in the Greek army or who deserted the Greek army were deported to other parts of Greece.[135] Then in 1924, Greece and Bulgaria signed a protocol placing the Macedonian minority in Greece under protection of the League of Nations.[136] But for ethnic Macedonians who were either expelled or who had left voluntarily, Greece could still lease their lands to resettled Greeks from Turkey and other parts of Greece without payment to the Macedonians; or if the settlers wanted to remain permanently, Greece could give the Greek settlers the land, with payment going to the ethnic Macedonian owners in due time.[137]

This treaty was short-lived, as in 1925 the Greeks withdrew from the treaty, and all Macedonians were regarded as Greek.[138] The Venizelos Doctrine against Macedonians then attempted to create a homogenous Greek population.[139] Land and property owned by ethnic Macedonians was impounded and confiscated by the Greeks;[140] and up until World War II, the Greek government encouraged Greeks from other parts of Greece to move north to Aegean Macedonia.[141] Over 600,000 ethnic Greeks had resettled the area since 1913.[142]

To the north, "the Serbian authorities tried to repress every trace of the Macedonian nationalist sentiment."[143] Macedonians under Serbian occupation had to Serbianize their names, similar to the Macedonians living in Greece who were forced to end their surnames in '-os' or '-is'.[144] Serbian efforts to Serbianize the Macedonians somewhat diminished after Macedonians prevailed through utilization of strong messages of refusal, such as when the Macedonian IMRO "massacred thirty colonists" sent by Serbia to settle in Vardar Macedonia.[145]

For Greece, however, these similar name-changing tactics were part of an assimilation and Hellenization plan for the ethnic Macedonian people in Greece.[146] The government changed town and people's names to Greek, in addition to the place names of rivers and mountains;[147] local authorities altered religious icons; and the government ordered all religious services to be performed in Greek.[148] The English journalist V. Hild described the Greek government's atrocities in Aegean Macedonia: "The Greeks do not only persecute living Slavs [Macedonians]…, but they even persecute dead ones. They do not leave them in peace even in the graves. They erase the Slavonic inscriptions on the

---

[135] *Id.*

[136] Underdown, Michael, *Background to the Macedonian Question*, 4 (1994).

[137] Kontogiorgi, Elisabeth, *Population Exchange in Greek Macedonia : The Forced Settlement of Refugees, 1922-1930*, 201 (2006).

[138] Underdown, Michael, *Background to the Macedonian Question*, 4 (1994).

[139] Apostolov, Mico, *The Macedonian Question -- Changes in Content Over Time*, vi (2006).

[140] Vankin, Sam, *Macedonia to the Macedonians,* (2000).

[141] Human Rights Watch, *Denying Ethnic Identity: The Macedonians in Greece*, 5 (1994).

[142] *Id.*

[143] Udovicki, Jasminka, *The Bonds and Fault Lines*, in *Burn This House: The Making and Unmaking of Yugoslavia*, 34 (1997).

[144] Apostolov, Mico, *The Macedonian Question -- Changes in Content Over Time*, vi (2006).

[145] Udovicki, Jasminka, *The Bonds and Fault Lines*, in *Burn This House: The Making and Unmaking of Yugoslavia*, 34 (1997).

[146] Human Rights Watch, *Denying Ethnic Identity: The Macedonians in Greece*, 5 (1994).

[147] Gay McDougall Mission to Greece, *Promotion and Protection of All Human Rights, Civil, Political, Economic, Social and Cultural Rights, Including the Right to Development*, 13 (2009).

[148] Human Rights Watch, *Denying Ethnic Identity: The Macedonians in Greece*, 6 (1994).

headstones, remove the bones and burn them."[149]

When the Metaxas dictatorship ruled Greece, Greek officials beat and fined people for speaking Macedonian, and all Macedonians were required to attend school to learn the Modern Greek language,[150] taught by specially trained instructors to accelerate the language conversion process.[151] Those Macedonians who refused to accept Greek as their mother tongue were exiled. All of this happened despite a 1930 statement by then Greek Prime Minister Eleaterios Venizelos proclaiming that "[t]he problem of a Macedonian minority will be solved and I will be the first one to commit myself to the opening of Macedonian schools if the nation so wishes."[152] An Australian author in 1938 explained these tragedies facing Macedonians:

> If Greece has no Jewish problem, she has the Macedonians. In the name of "Hellenization" these people are being persecuted continually and arrested for the most fantastic reasons. Metaxas' way of inculcating the proper nationalist spirit among them has been to change all the native place-names into Greek and to forbid use of the native language. For displaying the slightest resistance to this edict - for this too is a danger to the security of the State - peasants and villagers have been exiled without trial. [153]

Meanwhile, the Macedonians in Bulgaria, primarily in Pirin Macedonia, still strived for autonomy.[154] Myron Weiner describes how the Macedonians struggled for freedom between World War I and World War II:

> In the 1920's the Internal Macedonian Revolutionary Organization (IMRO) took control of a portion of Macedonia lying within Bulgaria, known as the Petrich Department, and assumed considerable power within the Bulgarian government. IMRO had its major support from immigrants who had fled into Bulgaria during the Balkan wars and who provided a reservoir of manpower on which IMRO could draw for its terrorist cadres. IMRO engaged in terrorist acts and assassinations in both Yugoslavia and Bulgaria, and deliberately sought to keep the region in such a state of unrest that news of it would constantly appear in the world press, so that the great powers would feel forced to redraw the Balkan frontiers. IMRO played a major role in overthrowing the Peasant Union government of Prime Minister Stamboliski, who had sought a rapprochement with Yugoslavia and had attempted to curb IMRO by arresting its leaders. IMRO leaders personally executed the Prime Minister. Throughout the 1920's and early thirties IMRO continued to engage in assassinations and terrorism within Bulgaria and to exercise great influence at the highest levels of government. In a reaction foreshadowing the behavior of the Jordanian army in 1970, in 1934 the Bulgarian military launched a coup, dismissed parliament, dissolved all political parties, censored the press, and suppressed IMRO.[155]

The Macedonians, fighting for rights and a United Macedonia, "terrorized the region with

---

[149] Medichkov, Peter, *Greek Acts Against the Macedonians: 1912-1994*, http://maknews.com/html/articles/medichkov/medichkov_report.htm .
[150] Human Rights Watch, *Denying Ethnic Identity: The Macedonians in Greece*, 6 (1994).
[151] Medichkov, Peter, *Greek Acts Against the Macedonians: 1912-1994*, http://maknews.com/html/articles/medichkov/medichkov_report.htm .
[152] *The Human Rights Situation of Macedonians in Greece and Australia*, http://www.pollitecon.com/html/life/The_Human_Rights_Situation_of_Macedonians_in_Greece_and_Australia.html . Jul. 1993.
[153] *Id.*
[154] Apostolov, Mico, *The Macedonian Question -- Changes in Content Over Time*, vii (2006).
[155] Weiner, Myron, *The Macedonian Syndrome: An Historical Model of International Relations and Political Development*, 23 World Politics 4, 678-9 (1971).

assassinations and cross-border raids,"[156] as they had very few legitimate political means to achieve any of their objectives. The "bandit king" of these Macedonians was Ivan Mihailoff, who not only ordered the assassinations of Bulgarians against Macedonia's independence struggle, but also of fellow Macedonians[157] that were presumably deemed traitors to the Macedonian struggle. Eventually, Mihailoff escaped to Turkey after being declared an outlaw by the Bulgarian government.[158]

During World War II, many Bulgarians worked alongside the Nazis and attempted to Bulgarianize the Macedonians,[159] as Bulgaria occupied most of geographic Macedonia during the war. Leaders and members of a Macedonian organization operating within Bulgaria that wanted to reestablish a united Macedonia were executed by the Bulgarian communists, even though the Macedonian organization was political and non-violent.[160] The Macedonians were eventually victorious in Vardar Macedonia, in the end, as the 100,000-strong Macedonian army sacrificed 24,000 Macedonian lives to defeat the occupiers, without the military aid of the Allied Powers.[161]

In 1946, shortly after the war and a year after Macedonian became an officially internationally recognized language, Tito created six republics within Yugoslavia, of which one was the People's Republic of Macedonia.[162] Writing eight years after this success for Macedonia and Macedonians, Stoyan Christowe (once a legislator for the US state of Vermont), described the effect this had for Macedonians:

> Until eight years ago, the Macedonians were a people but not a nation; they had a homeland, but not a country; and they spoke a distinct Slavic tongue which never had been recognized as a language. They had no universities, schools, newspapers, magazines, museums, no monument or any other kind of institution which goes toward making up a nation. The history of Macedonia was one of foreign oppression, terror and assassination.[163]

However, Macedonians still longed for a unified and independent Macedonia. In order to quell this Macedonian aspiration for independence, the Community Party of Yugoslavia "declared all … independence-seekers to be pro-Bulgarian enemies of the federation," and imprisoned those who talked about such desires.[164]

The Greek Civil War in the 1940s triggered massive numbers of ethnic Macedonians and Greek Communists to flee from Greece to Yugoslavia. The roots of the Macedonian involvement can be dated to the division of Macedonia in 1913, but more proximately, to the axis occupation of geographic Macedonia.[165] The Greek communist

---

[156] Simons, Marlise, *For the Name of Macedonia, a Burst of Greek Pride,*
http://select.nytimes.com/gst/abstract.html?res=F10615FA3C5E0C748DDDAD0894DA494D81 Apr. 17, 1992.
[157] Fowler, Glenn, *Ivan Mihailoff Dies in Rome at 94; Macedonian Rebel in Futile Fight,*
http://select.nytimes.com/gst/abstract.html?res=F30611FA3F5C0C758CDDA00894D8494D81 . Sep. 6th, 1990.
[158] *Id.*
[159] Kaplan, Robert D., *Balkan Ghosts: A Journey Throughout History,* 66 (1993).
[160] Shea, John, *Macedonia and Greece: The Struggle to Define a New Nation,* 172.
[161] *Id.* at177.
[162] *Id.* at 176.
[163] Christowe, Stoyan, *Macedonians Struggle to Develop as Nation,* <u>The Calgary Herald</u>, Feb. 18, 1953 (23).
[164] Shea, John, *Macedonia and Greece: The Struggle to Define a New Nation,* 178.
[165] Van Meter, David C., *The Macedonian Question and the Guerrilla War in Northern Greece on the Eve of*

party (KKE), fighting against the British-backed Greek royalists and monarchists,[166] helped form the Slavic Popular Liberation Front (composed of the ethnic Macedonians); but these two groups had conflicting interests, as the Macedonians wanted autonomy, and the KKE wanted to gain control over Greece.[167] In 1944, the Macedonian National Assembly "called for all Macedonians [...] to arise together and expel the Germans in order to establish a unified Macedonia" two months after its symbolic creation on August 2nd.[168] As a matter of fact, the "commander-in-chief of the Macedonian Partisan forces told an OSS liaison officer that the unification of Macedonia was certain[.]"[169] "These developments were noted with alarm by the Anglo-American powers, [...] [t]he British and Americans speculated that the Soviets might use the issue of Macedonian autonomy as cover for a push to gain access to the Aegean Sea."[170] For these reasons, the US Secretary of State at the time, Edward Stettinius, Jr., "condemned any reference to a Macedonian 'fatherland' or 'national conscience.'"[171]

Some estimate that nearly 40% of the KKE's troops were Macedonians.[172,173] The US State Department intelligence found that "the insurrection was dominated by Macedonian separatists even after the ... KKE assumed an active role in directing the fighting in late 1946."[174] The US estimated that over half of these fighters were ethnic Macedonians while only one-fifth of them were members of the KKE.[175] From 1947 until mid-1949, the ethnic Macedonian fighters increased from just over 5,000 to about 14,000.[176] But the Macedonians still needed the support and success of the KKE for a Macedonian victory.[177]

The Yugoslavs and some Western observers noted that "[e]nforcement of simple minority rights for schools and culture" for the Macedonian minority in Greece would have solved most of the 'Macedonian problems'.[178] As Dusan Sinadinoski points out, "...Greece's domestic policy [was] the root cause of the plight of refugees and the discrimination against the Macedonian minority."[179] He points to "a secret telegram to US

---

the Truman Doctrine, Journal of the Hellenic Diaspora, 74.

[166] Smith, Helena, *Bittersweet Return for Greek Civil War's Lost Victims: Greece is Allowing Ethnic Macedonians Exiled in the 1940s to Revisit Their Homes for the First Time,* http://www.guardian.co.uk/world/2003/oct/17/greece . Oct. 17, 2003.

[167] Van Meter, David C., *The Macedonian Question and the Guerrilla War in Northern Greece on the Eve of the Truman Doctrine,* Journal of the Hellenic Diaspora, 74.

[168] *Id.* at 75.

[169] *Id.*

[170] *Id.* at 76.

[171] Simons, Marlise, *For the Name of Macedonia, a Burst of Greek Pride,* http://select.nytimes.com/gst/abstract.html?res=F10615FA3C5E0C748DDDAD0894DA494D81 Apr. 17, 1992.

[172] Underdown, Michael, *Background to the Macedonian Question,* 5 (1994).

[173] International Crisis Group, *Macedonia's Name: Breaking the Deadlock,* 3 (2009).

[174] Van Meter, David C., *The Macedonian Question and the Guerrilla War in Northern Greece on the Eve of the Truman Doctrine,* Journal of the Hellenic Diaspora, 71.

[175] *Id.*

[176] Rossos, Andrew, *Incompatible Allies: Greek Communism and Macedonian Nationalism in the Civil War in Greece, 1943-1949,* 69 The Journal of Modern History 1, 1997: 44.

[177] *Id.* at 43.

[178] De Luce, Daniel, *Macedonia Fears Another War But Prays for Peace,* The Palm Beach Post, Aug. 25, 1947: 6.

[179] Sinadinoski, Dusan, *1947 UN Commission Established the Existence of the Macedonian Minority in Greece,* http://maknews.com/html/articles/sinadinoski/1947_UN_Commission_Macedonia.html 2008.

Secretary of State"[180] by Mark Ethridge:

> Greece itself by its own short sighted attitude and by its discriminatory and gangster-like methods was providing grist for the mill of political indoctrination and training in northern countries. It is noteworthy that a very large proportion of the refugees from Greece are Slavo-Macedonians who bore the brunt of discrimination. It seems clear to me that unless the discriminatory treatment stops flight to the mountains or across the borders will not stop. Thus this is the interrelation between nature and the causes and conclusion that Greece's discrimination has caused thousands to flee.[181]

But under Greek dictatorship, enforcing minority rights would not happen; thus, the Macedonians had no choice but to fight against this discrimination and to unite geographical Macedonia into Yugoslavia,[182] as "400,000 of their brethren were in nearby territory under Greek and Bulgarian rule."[183] These intentions and benefits are summed up by L. Damovski:

> The desire of Aegean Macedonia is Unification with Free Macedonia in accordance with the principles of the Atlantic Charter and the declarations of Stalin-Roosevelt-Churchill.... The Greek people have nothing to lose from such Unification.... The common struggle of the Macedonians and the Greeks will help open the way for the unification of the Macedonians with free Macedonia; for the Greeks [it] will win democracy, throw over the foreign yoke, and pave the way for people's rule in Greece.[184]

As a matter of fact, Yugoslavia and Bulgaria had already come to an agreement to unite Vardar Macedonia with Pirin Macedonia, and were simply awaiting the right moment to include Aegean Macedonia in this endeavor.[185] The *London Times* even reported that in August 1946, the Bulgarian and Yugoslav governments met with the Greek communists to unite Aegean Macedonia with Pirin and Vardar Macedonia.[186] But as indicated in one journalist's account of his visit to Vardar Macedonia after the first year of fighting in the Greek Civil War, nothing suggested that Macedonians in Yugoslavia, or Yugoslavia itself, was aiding or going to aid the Macedonians in Greece with military support:

> The only mobilization I could see here is to better public health and eradicate illiteracy. Posters in the wayside taverns urge the peasants to drain malarial pools and enroll in classes for A.B.C. [...] We motored through territory which critics of Yugoslavia have insinuated was an arsenal and training camp for forces fighting the Greek army on the other side of the border. What we saw was a panorama of peaceful development. Allied military representatives who visited this area recently likewise report finding no evidence that Macedonia is stirring up fire of revolt in Greece. [...] In Bitolj, 12 miles from Hellenic soil and astride the 'Monastir Gap' through which the Germans invaded Greece in 1941, the biggest topic of local conversation is the Macedonian bricklayer Velo Belovski. [...]

---

[180] *Id.*

[181] *Id.*

[182] International Crisis Group, *Macedonia's Name: Breaking the Deadlock*, 3 (2009).

[183] De Luce, Daniel, *Macedonia Fears Another War But Prays for Peace*, The Palm Beach Post, Aug. 25, 1947: 6.

[184] Rossos, Andrew, *Incompatible Allies: Greek Communism and Macedonian Nationalism in the Civil War in Greece, 1943-1949*, 69 The Journal of Modern History 1, 1997: 55.

[185] Van Meter, David C., *The Macedonian Question and the Guerrilla War in Northern Greece on the Eve of the Truman Doctrine*, Journal of the Hellenic Diaspora, 77.

[186] *Id.* at 79-80.

Talking with officials and private citizens alike, we found none who said they wanted Macedonia to expand its frontiers at the expense of Greece. Some remarked that the Macedonian minority in Greece was now undergoing 'a tragedy of terror at the hands of monarcho-fascists.' But they expressed no animosity toward the Greek people. They said Salonika was a Greek populated city and they knew of no reason to claim it for Macedonia in the future. [...] Macedonians plainly seem more interested in agricultural prices than in the details of international disputes.[187]

In another article, the same author stated that "[i]t [was] a fact that British and American diplomatic and military observers in Yugoslavia [were] repeatedly embarrassed by the fanciful rumors planted in the world press by Greek government spokesmen."[188]

Still, conflicting reports emerged over Yugoslavia's role. In late 1946, Greece accused Yugoslavia of shooting down a Greek airplane.[189] However, Yugoslavian news reported that the Greek aircraft had invaded Yugoslav airspace, and thus Yugoslavia shot it down, and then repelled two other Greek warplanes that were "attempt[ing] to destroy the downed plane 'in order to obliterate evidence of violation of Yugoslav territory.'"[190] What is most likely true regarding Yugoslavia's involvement is that Yugoslavia was politically active in liberating occupied Macedonia. Because Macedonians were a people and a nation of Yugoslavia, and because many Macedonians were connected to their homelands in Greece and Bulgaria, Yugoslavia simply supported its people and the freedom of these Macedonians in Greece and Bulgaria. However, there is no doubt that a free Aegean Macedonia would have benefited Tito's Yugoslavia, both economically and politically.

Actually, Yugoslavia did not hide the fact that they supported a Macedonia for the Macedonians. The Yugoslav delegate, Moisha Pijade, voiced Yugoslavia's stance at a peace conference in 1946: "It is time to settle this question of the liberty of the Macedonian people. The people, until now, have found their liberty only in the popular republic of Macedonia within the Macedonian Yugoslav federation."[191] He added that Macedonia was a place which "ha[d] always been a principal cause of Balkan quarrels."[192] The Yugoslav ambassador to the United States, Sava N. Kasanovich, reaffirmed this position later in December of 1946, when the UN decided to send a multi-national group to investigate claims of border violations between Greece and Yugoslavia:

I must categorically affirm that it is untrue that Yugoslavia is menacing the territorial integrity of Greece[.] [...] But it is obvious that the sympathies of the Yugoslav peoples, and especially of the Macedonian people, go to their opposed brothers in Aegean Macedonia, and that the sufferings of the Macedonians in Greece cannot fail to arouse a response in Yugoslavia.[193]

Much of this talk by the Yugoslavs was actually provoked by Greece's territorial ambitions. As one reporter reported in 1945:

[187] De Luce, Daniel, *Macedonia Likes Tito Rule: People Not After Greek Territory*, The Windsor Daily Star, Aug. 8, 1947: 21.

[188] De Luce, Daniel, *Macedonia Fears Another War But Prays for Peace*, The Palm Beach Post, Aug. 25, 1947: 6.

[189] Tension Increases Over Macedonia. The Leader Post. Sep. 7, 1946: 1.

[190] *Id.*

[191] *Id.*

[192] *Id.*

[193] Ryan, William L., *United States Suggest UN Send Group to Balkins to Sift Greek Border Charge*, Kentucky New Era, Dec. 18th, 1946: 1.

Constantly tightening the tension between Greece and Yugoslavia is the expansionist program favored by many highly placed Greeks, which would add to the Greek nation sizable lumps of territory from each of Greece's neighbors. The program would add most of Macedonia to Greece and would take over at least half of Albania. This naturally makes the neighbors angry.[194]

Still, just months earlier in September of 1946, the president of the Macedonian National Front, Dimitar Vlahov, "declared that Greece had no valid claim to Aegean Macedonia" in a press interview in Paris, and further stated that political unification of Macedonia was imminent.[195] In October, Tito said he was taking actions to stop the persecution of Macedonians in Greece.[196] A year earlier he had "accused Greek forces of firing across the Greek-Yugoslav border to 'provoke us' and said that thousands of Macedonians had fled Northern Greece to Yugoslavia to escape Greek terrorism."[197] Still, opposite to Greek claims, the US State Department found little evidence to support the claims that Yugoslavia was militarily supporting the Macedonian freedom fighters in Greece.[198] But even after the Macedonians and Greek communists gained control of most of Aegean Macedonia, the US backed, and helped reorganize, the Greek National Army.[199] Because of minimal support from the governments of Bulgaria and Yugoslavia, and the eventual resurgence of the Greek army, Macedonians were defeated in their attempt to free and unite Macedonia. The last effort to realize Macedonian independence occurred on the radio station "Fear Greece" in 1949, when an Independent United Macedonia was declared.[200] This attempt unfortunately failed.

One devastating result of this civil war for the Macedonians was that "[e]very household ha[d] a wounded or a dead [member]."[201] The horrors that Macedonians faced was incomprehensible: the Greek terror that haunted the Macedonians was "comparable in savagery with 'the most horrible in the times of Turkish enslavery.'"[202] The "[m]ethods that Greeks have been using to clear their side of the frontier of [Macedonian] dissident elements can have no justification," reported one journalist.[203] A popular tactic by the Greeks was forced expulsions, which when combined with "voluntary emigration," triggered up to 213,000 ethnic Macedonians to flee Aegean Macedonia,[204] of which an

---

[194] King, William B., *Trouble is Brewing in the Balkans*, The Milwaukee Journal, Jul. 29th, 1945: 46.

[195] Van Meter, David C., *The Macedonian Question and the Guerrilla War in Northern Greece on the Eve of the Truman Doctrine*, Journal of the Hellenic Diaspora, 80.

[196] *Id.*

[197] *Tito Charges Greek Terrorism on Macedonians: Sacking of Villages, Firing Over Border Laid to Fascists*, The Calgary Hearld, Jul. 9th, 1945: 7.

[198] Van Meter, David C., *The Macedonian Question and the Guerrilla War in Northern Greece on the Eve of the Truman Doctrine*, Journal of the Hellenic Diaspora, 88.

[199] Smith, Helena, *Bittersweet Return for Greek Civil War's Lost Victims: Greece is Allowing Ethnic Macedonians Exiled in the 1940s to Revisit Their Homes for the First Time*, http://www.guardian.co.uk/world/2003/oct/17/greece . Oct. 17, 2003.

[200] Poulton, Hugh, *The Balkans: Minorities and States in Conflict*, 178 (1994).

[201] Rossos, Andrew, *Incompatible Allies: Greek Communism and Macedonian Nationalism in the Civil War in Greece, 1943-1949*, 69 The Journal of Modern History 1, 1997: 44.

[202] *Tito Charges Greek Terrorism on Macedonians: Sacking of Villages, Firing Over Border Laid to Fascists*, The Calgary Hearld, Jul. 9th, 1945: 7.

[203] King, William B., *Trouble is Brewing in the Balkans*, The Milwaukee Journal, Jul. 29th, 1945: 46.

[204] Human Rights Watch, *Denying Ethnic Identity: The Macedonians in Greece*, 7 (1994).

estimated 30,000 were children.[205] Those who voluntarily fled did so because "Greek bands reportedly were plundering the countryside, robbing, raping, and driving [Macedonians] from their homes[.]"[206] Between 1945 and 1947, the Democratic Greek army reported that "in Western Macedonia [part of Aegean Macedonia] alone[,] 13,529 Macedonians were tortured, 3,215 were imprisoned and 268 were executed without trial. In addition, 1,891 houses were burnt down; 1,553 were looted; and 13,808 Macedonians were resettled by force."[207] If not forced to leave, Macedonians felt that they had no choice but to leave.

Under a Greek decree in 1953, Macedonians who fled were to be deprived of property and citizenship unless they returned within 3 years[208] (even though a 1948 United Nations resolution called for the repartition of the children refugees),[209] and Aegean Macedonia was colonized with "new colonists with healthy [Greek] national consciousness."[210] This resulted in the confiscation of many ethnic Macedonians' properties.[211] The year after, the Greek government removed all ethnic Macedonians from official government positions.[212] In 1959, Greek villages required Macedonian villagers to take a language oath to renounce their Slavic dialect and to only speak Greek, both in public and private.[213] Not being able to cope with the discrimination, many Macedonians from Aegean Macedonia again fled to Australia and Canada.[214]

Although Macedonians were not part of a civil war in Bulgaria during this time, the decades after World War II showed disturbing trends for them, especially in Pirin Macedonia. These trends amounted to what Loring Danforth describes as forced assimilation.[215] In 1946, it is estimated that there were over 250,000 Macedonians in Bulgaria; in 1956, just under 190,000; and ten years later the Bulgarian census reported only 8,750 Macedonians in Bulgaria.[216] Could it be that over 240,000 Macedonians had left Bulgaria in 20 years? Bulgaria was a nation who, at the turn of the 20th century, had a capitol of whose population was half Macedonian,[217] with further over 16,000 Macedonians living in tents outside of the capitol.[218] Then, in a century, Bulgaria transformed into a nation with virtually no Macedonians, according to the above statistics. The truth is that many Macedonians were, and still are, there; but they were just not

[205] Poulton, Hugh, *The Balkans: Minorities and States in Conflict*, 180 (1994).
[206] *Tito Charges Greek Terrorism on Macedonians: Sacking of Villages, Firing Over Border Laid to Fascists*, The Calgary Hearld, Jul. 9th, 1945: 7.
[207] *The Human Rights Situation of Macedonians in Greece and Australia*, http://www.pollitecon.com/html/life/The_Human_Rights_Situation_of_Macedonians_in_Greece_and_Australia.html . Jul. 1993.
[208] Underdown, Michael, *Background to the Macedonian Question*, 5 (1994).
[209] Medichkov, Peter, *Greek Acts Against the Macedonians: 1912-1994*, http://maknews.com/html/articles/medichkov/medichkov_report.htm .
[210] Poulton, Hugh, *The Balkans: Minorities and States in Conflict*, 178 (1994).
[211] International Crisis Group, *Macedonia's Name: Breaking the Deadlock*, 3 (2009).
[212] Poulton, Hugh, *The Balkans: Minorities and States in Conflict*, 179 (1994).
[213] Human Rights Watch, *Denying Ethnic Identity: The Macedonians in Greece*, 7 (1994).
[214] Poulton, Hugh, *The Balkans: Minorities and States in Conflict*, 179(1994).
[215] Danforth, Loring, *Claims to Macedonian Identity: The Macedonian Question and the Breakup of Yugoslavia*, 9 Anthropology Today 4, Aug. 1993: 4.
[216] Poulton, Hugh, *The Balkans: Minorities and States in Conflict*, 107 (1994).
[217] Mungiu-Pippidi, Alina, *Failed Institutional Transfer? Constraints on the Political Modernization of the Balkan, Ottomans into Europeans: State and Institution Building in South Eastern Europe*, 71 (2010).
[218] Kaplan, Robert D., *Balkan Ghosts: A Journey Throughout History*, 64 (1993).

counted as Macedonians, as demonstrated by the political happenings of the time. When Georgi Dimitrov led Bulgaria after World War II, the Macedonians was recognized as a separate ethnic group.[219] After 1956, Todor Zhivkov came to power and Bulgaria no longer recognized the Macedonians.[220]

The 1950s were also a decade of tense fear and speculation regarding the Macedonian issue on the entire Balkan Peninsula. This excerpt from 1993 in *The Calgary Herald* explains the sentiment:

> Macedonia may now attempt to press claims against Greece and Bulgaria for the sections of the country now under their jurisdiction in an attempt to unite the entire Macedonian race into a republic. This was in fact the case from 1945 until Yugoslavia was expelled from the commform in 1948, with the Macedonian district of Bulgaria little more than an extension of the Macedonian republic. The republic, however, being a sovereign state, is still an indivisible part of Yugoslavia and has no right or might to engage in war. The people know that their future is tied in with the future of Yugoslavia. There is agitation on the part of the commform neighbors to sever the republic from the Yugoslav body politic to be united with the parts under Greece and Bulgaria into an integral, 'independent' unit in the Balkan federation of soviet republics; but a plan such as this would not aid the republic, and would simply turn the clock back, leaving the Macedonian people where they were ten years ago.[221]

In the 1960s, a few years after Tito and his Yugoslav government officially recognized the Macedonian Orthodox Church,[222] the Macedonian Orthodox Church became "the most patriotic religious organization in the country."[223] Much of this probably had to do with the impossibility Macedonians had in establishing their own religious institution throughout several centuries of foreign occupation.[224] The 1960s in Bulgaria also saw the beginnings of movements by the Bulgarian government and historians to claim "the Macedonian revolutionary movement" of the late 1800s and early 1900s as part of Bulgarian history, after spending several decades trying to distance itself from that very same movement.[225] This actually sparked a heated showdown between Bulgaria and Yugoslavia in the late 1960s. In early 1968, Miso Pavicevic, the Yugoslavian foreign minister at the time, summoned the Bulgarian Ambassador "to protest a mounting Bulgarian press campaign which the Yugoslavs interpret[ed] as a renewal of Bulgarian claims to Macedonia."[226] Aside from arguing that the Macedonians were really Bulgarian, the Bulgarians were referencing a 90 year old peace treaty which, at that time, gave to Bulgaria all of Macedonia.[227]

In 1970, Bulgaria refused to sign three agreements with Yugoslavia because they were written in Macedonian, which was an official language of Yugoslavia.[228] In March of 1972, Soviet Defense Minister Andrei Grechko visited Vardar Macedonia in a symbolic

---

[219] Poulton, Hugh, *The Balkans: Minorities and States in Conflict*, 108 (1994).
[220] *Id.*
[221] Christowe, Stoyan, *Macedonians Struggle to Develop as Nation*, The Calgary Herald, Feb. 18, 1953 (23).
[222] Shea, John, *Macedonia and Greece: The Struggle to Define a New Nation*, 174.
[223] Perica, Vjekoslav, *Balkan Idols: Religion and Nationalism in Yugoslav States*, 12 (2002).
[224] Shea, John, *Macedonia and Greece: The Struggle to Define a New Nation*, 173-74.
[225] Frusetta, James, *Common Heroes, Divided Claims: IMRO Between Macedonia and Bulgaria*, in *Ideologies and National Identities : The Case of Twentieth-Century Southeastern Europe*, 113-113 (2003).
[226] Newsom, Phil, *Macedonian Tribal Feud Still Burns*, Sarasota Journal, Feb. 1st, 1968: 14.
[227] *Id.*
[228] *Macedonian Question is Still Vexing*, Reading Eagle. Aug. 13th, 1972: 36.

attempt to mute Bulgaria's territorial claims to Macedonia.[229] The 1970s were also a time of troubles for Macedonians within Bulgaria. In 1973, numerous Macedonians were sentenced to lengthy prison sentences for promoting Macedonian patriotism.[230] In 1974, Bulgaria infuriated Macedonians in geographic Macedonia and worldwide, along with the Yugoslav government, when it published an encyclopedia suggesting the Macedonians were racially Bulgarian and further presented the Macedonian issue with mistaken facts.[231] Then in 1976, a law was passed in Bulgaria which resulted in the forced resettlement of Macedonians from ethnic Macedonian communities to other regions of Bulgaria.[232]

The 1980s witnessed Greece passing laws only allowing ethnic Greeks to resettle and reclaim property.[233] Some of these policies stemmed from a 1982 "confidential report by the security branch of the Greek police" containing "highly controversial and inhuman recommendations about strategies to deal with the Macedonian problem'[.]"[234] These strategies included: wiping out the use of the Macedonian language; only placing people who refused to recognize the Macedonian language into public service and education positions; the establishment of "enlightenment seminars" to educate those who were receptive of the Macedonian language and cause; boosting Greek national sentiment by establishing pro-Greek cultural associations in Aegean Macedonia; creating obstacles for those Greeks who wanted to study in the People's Republic of Macedonia in Yugoslavia; intimidating villagers who were champions of Macedonian rights issues; and encouraging Greek army members to marry and assimilate Macedonian women.[235] The following year, Greece refused to recognize university degrees from the People's Republic of Macedonia because Greece did not recognize the Macedonian language.[236] The year after, in 1984, the 'Movement for Human and National Rights for the Macedonians of Aegean Macedonia,' operating in Greece, "issued a Manifest for Macedonian Human Rights" which stated that "[i]n Greece human rights are openly disregarded and our human existence is cursed. We, in the Aegean Macedonia, are determined to carry our struggle on various levels, employing all legal means until our rights are guaranteed."[237] Greece started protesting to the Pope in the Vatican and the US Ambassador to Yugoslavia for using the Macedonian language; and PEN, an international writer's organization, wrote in opposition to these Greek denials of the Macedonian language.[238] In 1988, Greece officially renamed its 'Northern Greece' province to 'Macedonia'.[239] It was also in the 1980s that Greek experts

[229] Djuric, Nesho, *Macedonia Remains Balkan Sore Spot*, Beaver County Times, Aug. 8th, 1972: 5.
[230] Poulton, Hugh, *The Balkans: Minorities and States in Conflict*, 109 (1994).
[231] *Yugoslavia Still Has Several Neighbor Problems With Trieste*, Ludington Daily News, Jun. 13, 1974: 10.
[232] Poulton, Hugh, *The Balkans: Minorities and States in Conflict*, 108 (1994).
[233] Human Rights Watch, *Denying Ethnic Identity: The Macedonians in Greece*, 9 (1994).
[234] *The Human Rights Situation of Macedonians in Greece and Australia*, http://www.pollitecon.com/html/life/The_Human_Rights_Situation_of_Macedonians_in_Greece_and_Aust ralia.html . Jul. 1993.
[235] National Security Service. Protocol 6502/7-3042. Feb. 16, 1982: Athens. http://www.maknews.com/forum/post220073.html
[236] *The Human Rights Situation of Macedonians in Greece and Australia*, http://www.pollitecon.com/html/life/The_Human_Rights_Situation_of_Macedonians_in_Greece_and_Aust ralia.html . Jul. 1993.
[237] *Id.*
[238] *Id.*
[239] Axt, Heinz-Jurgen et. al., *The Greek Macedonian Name Dispute -- Reconciliation through Europeanization?*, 10 (2006).

coined the phrase 'Macedonia is Greek', which suggested to the Europeans that Greece had territorial ambitions toward the People's Republic of Macedonia.[240]

However, several ethnic Greeks within Greece fought against these systematic human rights violations against Macedonians in Aegean Macedonia during the same time period. A Greek newspaper wrote that the Macedonian minority did exist in Greece; leaders of the Greek Communist party acknowledged that Greece had an ethnic Macedonian minority; an Athenian monthly journal published articles demanding the halt of ethnic discrimination on Macedonians, claiming ethnic Macedonians were the Palestinians of Europe; and nearly 100 Greek intellectuals, in a note of protest, spoke out against the Greek government for such abuses.[241] The Greek government and Europe ignored much of this.

Mass demonstrations rocked the People's Republic of Macedonia in the early 1990s, as protesters demanded a halt to the suppression of, and more rights for, the Macedonian minority in Greece.[242] This eventually led to a revision in the People's Republic of Macedonia's constitution stating that the Republic of Macedonia must look after the rights of Macedonians in neighboring countries.[243] Much of this was in reaction to the soon-to-be Greek Prime Minister Constantine Mitsotakis' statement denying the existence of Macedonians in Greece: "[w]e are clean because Greece is the only Balkan country without the problem of national minorities. [...] The Macedonian minority does not exist[.]"[244]

During Tito's Yugoslavia, Greece did not seem bothered by the fact that a Macedonia existed in Yugoslavia. After all, the Greek portion of Macedonia during this time was not even referred to as Macedonia. It could even be said that Greece strived to hide and deny the existence of Macedonia. However, this Greek attitude quickly changed when Macedonia became an independent country.

4. The era of negotiations

In the late 1980s and early 1990s, the nations and peoples of Yugoslavia were confronted with sharp economic, political and ethnic divisions, thanks in part to mismanagement of the country after Tito's death. Most of the country spiraled into chaos and a devastating war. Fortunately, the Republic of Macedonia avoided the bloodshed that ensued through the first half of the decade. This was partly possible because of the proactive stances the international community took with the People's Republic of Macedonia compared to the rest of Yugoslavia. For example, the only ex-Yugoslav state to

---

[240] Kofos, Evangelos, *Greece's Macedonian Adventure: The Controversy over FYROM's Independence and Recognition*, 3.

[241] *The Human Rights Situation of Macedonians in Greece and Australia*, http://www.pollitecon.com/html/life/The_Human_Rights_Situation_of_Macedonians_in_Greece_and_Australia.html . Jul. 1993.

[242] Axt, Heinz-Jurgen et. al., *The Greek Macedonian Name Dispute -- Reconciliation through Europeanization?*, 9 (2006).

[243] *Id.*

[244] *The Human Rights Situation of Macedonians in Greece and Australia*, http://www.pollitecon.com/html/life/The_Human_Rights_Situation_of_Macedonians_in_Greece_and_Australia.html . Jul. 1993.

which the United States initially sent troops was the People's Republic of Macedonia, as they feared a war there would have engulfed the entire Balkan region, especially after the CIA warned that a Serbian attack on the People's Republic of Macedonia was imminent.[245] A war in the People's Republic of Macedonia would have consisted of all Macedonia's neighbors and Turkey, which would have been the first time that two NATO countries (Greece and Turkey) participated in an armed conflict against one another.[246]

On September 8, 1991, Macedonians went to the polls to vote for independence.[247] About three-fourths of the People's Republic of Macedonia's citizens came out to vote,[248] with most of the non-voters consisting of ethnic Albanians who boycotted the vote. Nearly 96% of the voters voted for independence and on September 17th, the People's Republic of Macedonia proclaimed its independence[249] as the Republic of Macedonia. Around the same time, Greece began advocating that this "new Macedonian republic" should be incorporated into Greece.[250] The Greek Post Office began issuing stamps, plastered with ancient Macedonian and Byzantine Macedonian references, which stated "Macedonia is and always will be Greek."[251] It could even be said that "the Greek public went on a state of mass nationalist hysteria over the Macedonian issue."[252]

From the onset of declaring independence, Macedonia barely remained afloat. An uneasy large Albanian minority population threatened Macedonia's sovereignty; the fear of war in Bosnia and Croatia spreading south to Macedonia worried many people; and economic hardships plagued the Macedonians due to a Greek embargo to the south and world sanctions on Yugoslavia to the north.[253]

In December of 1991, the Council of Ministers of the European Community (EC) met in Brussels to discuss recognizing Macedonia.[254] The Greek foreign minister in attendance revealed Greece's fears of the propaganda originating in Macedonia regarding Macedonia's history, and he suggested that Macedonia might have territorial claims against Greece's northern territory.[255,256] He said this even though he and the world knew that Macedonia's "extremely poor, ill-equipped" military posed no threat to Greece.[257]

Greece also objected to several provisions in Macedonia's constitution.[258] The constitution contained supposed references to the annexation of Macedonian lands

[245] Paquin, Jonathan, *Managing Controversy: U.S. Stability Seeking and the Birth of the Macedonian State*, 447 (2008).
[246] Rossos, Andrew, *Macedonia and the Macedonians*. 271 (2008).
[247] Tziampiris, Aristotle, *The Name Dispute in the Former Yugoslav Republic of Macedonia After the Signing of the Interim Accord*, 226.
[248] *Id.*
[249] *Id.*
[250] Underdown, Michael, *Background to the Macedonian Question*, 6 (1994).
[251] Kofos, Evangelos, *Greece's Macedonian Adventure: The Controversy over FYROM's Independence and Recognition*, 3.
[252] Kostovilis, Spyridon, *Exploring the Sources of Greek Foreign Policy Towards the Former Yugoslav Republic of Macedonia*, 8 (2005).
[253] Floudas, Demetrius A., *Pardon? A Conflict for a Name?: Fyrom's Dispute with Greece Revisited*, 4.
[254] *Id.*
[255] *Id.*
[256] Vankin, Sam, *Gruevski's Macedonia, Greece, and Alexander the Great, History's Forgotten Madman*, (2009).
[257] Kostovilis, Spyridon, *Exploring the Sources of Greek Foreign Policy Towards the Former Yugoslav Republic of Macedonia*, 17 (2005).
[258] Floudas, Demetrius A., *Pardon? A Conflict for a Name?: Fyrom's Dispute with Greece Revisited*, 5.

conquered by Macedonia's neighbors in the early 1900s, and many Greeks believed it urged resistance against those countries who carved up Macedonia in the first place.[259] Specifically, the Greeks interpreted Article 49 to suggest that Macedonia could interfere in Greece's internal affairs in order to protect the Macedonian minority in Aegean Macedonia.[260] Because the Council was engrossed with the heightening ethnic escalation in Yugoslavia, it readily accepted Greece's positions.[261]

In the beginning of the next year, Greece sentenced six ethnic Macedonians to prison for distributing posters that asked citizens to recognize Macedonia.[262] Greece also charged an ethnic Macedonian Orthodox priest and human rights campaigner in Greece with "being a homosexual and a Skopjan spy" in order to publicly humiliate and harass him.[263] The mood throughout Greece at the time was mostly anti-Macedonian.

When the EC President offered a compromise in which Macedonia would promise to stop hostile propaganda, not pursue territorial claims, and accept 'New Macedonia' as the name, Macedonia was responsive to the first two points but remained noncommittal to the name, awaiting a Greek response.[264] The Greek Foreign Minister, Andonis Samaras, refused to accept the name, however.[265] Macedonia eventually made amendments to its constitution in order to appease most of Greece's demands.[266] The constitution was amended to state: "The Republic of Macedonia has no territorial claims against neighboring countries."[267] According to Robert Badinter, the leader of the Arbitration Commission of the EC, Macedonia thus "'satisfied the tests in the [EC] guidelines' for recognition."[268] Among the criteria necessary for such recognition included "the existence of a permanent population and a democratically elected, stable government with the ability to enter into relations with other sovereign states[,] […] [and] a constitution guaranteeing full political, social, cultural and religious rights to all citizens."[269]

But Greece still objected because they believed the sentiment about the prior constitutional positions still remained in Macedonia.[270] In February, Portugal held the presidency of the EC presidency and relayed that the name 'New Macedonia' could not be agreed on.[271] Shortly after, in April, President George Bush "reversed [the United States'] initial decision" to recognize Macedonia because the Republic of Macedonia could not prove that an "inter state war would [not] occur in Greece."[272]

---

[259] *Id.* at 5.

[260] *Id.*

[261] *Id.* at 4.

[262] Human Rights Watch, *Denying Ethnic Identity: The Macedonians in Greece*, 25 (1994).

[263] *The Human Rights Situation of Macedonians in Greece and Australia*, http://www.pollitecon.com/html/life/The_Human_Rights_Situation_of_Macedonians_in_Greece_and_Australia.html . Jul. 1993.

[264] Kofos, Evangelos, *Greece's Macedonian Adventure: The Controversy over FYROM's Independence and Recognition*, 5.

[265] *Id.*

[266] Floudas, Demetrius A., *Pardon? A Conflict for a Name?: Fyrom's Dispute with Greece Revisited*, 5.

[267] Underdown, Michael, *Background to the Macedonian Question*, 6 (1994).

[268] International Crisis Group, *Macedonia's Name: Why the Dispute Matters and How to Resolve It*, 12 (2001).

[269] Warne, Leslie, *We Exist, Say Illawarra Macedonians*, http://www.greenleft.org.au/node/2031 Mar. 11th, 1992.

[270] Floudas, Demetrius A., *Pardon? A Conflict for a Name?: Fyrom's Dispute with Greece Revisited*, 5.

[271] *Id.* at 4.

[272] Paquin, Jonathan, *Managing Controversy: U.S. Stability Seeking and the Birth of the Macedonian State*,

In May, thanks to a "vigorous [Greek] campaign against recognition,"[273] the EC stated that they would only recognize an independent and sovereign Macedonia under a name to which all interested parties could agree.[274] In June, the EC then announced that not only would it not accept the name 'Macedonia' for the new republic,[275] it would not recognize Macedonia "under a name which... include[d] the denomination Macedonia."[276] In July, Macedonia's government fell apart,[277] and the Macedonians responded to this injustice by electing more hardliners into office and adopting the ancient Macedonian 16-ray Vergina sun as its national flag.[278] Immediately, Macedonia applied for recognition from the UN.[279] Taking Macedonia's case to London, Macedonian Information Minister Martin Trenevski told reporters:

> 'The EC should bear in mind that social instability in Macedonia has already been the cause of two Balkan wars. It can very easily be the cause of a third one, and a much broader conflict.' [Trenevski] warned that Serbia, Bulgaria, Greece, Albania and Turkey could all be drawn in, and with that, the Muslim world ... 'This is a very good chance for British diplomacy to do something to prevent other conflicts[.]'[280]

And paraphrasing Shakespeare, Macedonia's US Representative Ljubica Acevska summed up Macedonia's dilemma by stating, "[y]ou take away my name, you take away my soul."[281]

In response to Macedonia's desire to be recognized as a country and as the Republic of Macedonia, Greece renamed its Thessaloniki airport from 'Micra' to 'Macedonia;'[282] the airport in Kavalla was renamed 'Alexander the Great;' and warships were 'rebaptized' with ancient Macedonian names.[283] Furthermore, the University of Thessaloniki was renamed to the University of Macedonia, Alexander the Great's image was plastered onto coins, the star of Vergina (Macedonia's national flag) was painted on all city buses, and that same symbol then was used to represent Greece's annexed portion of geographic Macedonia.[284] In a matter of a few years, Greek policies and actions managed

---

444 (2008).

[273] *Id.*

[274] Kofos, Evangelos, *Greece's Macedonian Adventure: The Controversy over FYROM's Independence and Recognition,* 6.

[275] Floudas, Demetrius A., *Pardon? A Conflict for a Name?: Fyrom's Dispute with Greece Revisited,* 4.

[276] Kofos, Evangelos, *Greece's Macedonian Adventure: The Controversy over FYROM's Independence and Recognition,* 6.

[277] *Macedonia is Denied Recognition,* The Rochester Sentinel, August 15th, 1992: 1.

[278] Floudas, Demetrius A., *Pardon? A Conflict for a Name?: Fyrom's Dispute with Greece Revisited,* 4.

[279] *Id.*

[280] Savill, Annika, *Macedonians Warn of War,*
http://www.independent.co.uk/news/world/europe/macedonians-warn-of-war-1533124.html . Jul. 14th, 1992.

[281] *Macedonia is Denied Recognition,* The Rochester Sentinel, August 15th, 1992: 1.

[282] *Macedonia: New Name for Thessaloniki airport,*
http://www.b92.net/eng/news/region-article.php?yyyy=2008&mm=07&dd=25&nav_id=52204 July 25, 2008.

[283] Simons, Marlise, *For the Name of Macedonia, a Burst of Greek Pride,*
http://select.nytimes.com/gst/abstract.html?res=F10615FA3C5E0C748DDDAD0894DA494D81 Apr. 17, 1992.

[284] Gerogevski, Borce, *The Real Reasons Why Greece is Opposed to the Name of Republic of Macedonia,*
http://www.pelagon.de/?p=1150 . Feb. 17th, 2009.

to change the views of a Greek population, which at one time refused to associate with anything Macedonian.

Still, in December of 1992, Macedonia's president Kiril Gligorov supported the plan by Special Representative of EC and British Ambassador Robin O'Neil to allow Macedonia to use 'Republic of Macedonia' for internal use and 'Republic of Macedonia (Skopje)' for international use.[285] But Greece rejected this proposal and stated that the term 'Macedonia' did not have any place in the newly independent country's name.[286] President Gligorov was subjected to many internal attacks for giving in to Greece's demands to the extent that he did.[287] Even with Gligorov's willingness to settle the dispute with a more-than-fair compromise for Greece, Greece continued to reject mediation attempts.[288]

In January 1993, Greece and Macedonia both sent memos to the UN stating how the other was trying to destabilize the region.[289] During the same time, France recommended that the dispute should be settled by international arbitration, where both Greece and Macedonia would had to have accepted the final result.[290] Macedonia did not favor this idea because it believed "its credentials ha[d] already been vetted and approved by the Badinter Commission," which had ruled the year before that Macedonia deserved recognition as a sovereign state.[291] Speaking about this issue at the UN in February, President Gligorov proclaimed:

> It is surprising that the Republic of Greece disputes article 49 of our Constitution which refers to the care of the Republic of Macedonia for our minority in the neighbouring countries. It should be pointed out that there is a similar provision in the Greek constitution. It is a well known fact that the Republic of Greece does not admit the existence of a Macedonian minority there.[292]

The next month, five OSCE members were arrested in Greece for publishing a document which spoke about the Macedonian Question.[293] A few months later, two Macedonian activists were sentenced to prison and fined for publicly stating that they felt Macedonian and for claiming that one million ethnic Macedonians live in Greece.[294] Gligorov's UN statement about the treatment of the Macedonian minorities was not without merit.

When Macedonia was recommended for admission into the UN on April 8th,[295]

---

[285] Tziampiris, Aristotle, *The Name Dispute in the Former Yugoslav Republic of Macedonia After the Signing of the Interim Accord*, 227.

[286] *Id.*

[287] *Id.* at 228.

[288] *Id.*

[289] *Id.*

[290] Lambert, Sarah, *Greek Refusal to Recognise Macedonia Comes Under Fire*, http://www.independent.co.uk/news/world/europe/greek-refusal-to-recognise-macedonia-comes-under-fire-1479801.html . Jan. 21st, 1993.

[291] *Id.*

[292] *The Human Rights Situation of Macedonians in Greece and Australia*, http://www.pollitecon.com/html/life/The_Human_Rights_Situation_of_Macedonians_in_Greece_and_Australia.html . Jul. 1993.

[293] *Id.*

[294] Human Rights Watch, *Denying Ethnic Identity: The Macedonians in Greece*, 24 (1994).

[295] Vangelov, Ognen, *The Greek Veto the Macedonian Identity*, 2.

Greece objected to the flying of the Macedonian flag at the UN building.[296] They objected so adamantly that the UN issued some additional conditions for UN membership, even though Article 4 of the UN Charter consists of an exhaustive list of the necessary prerequisites to become a member.[297] First, raising Macedonia's new flag would be deferred to a future date in order to protect "Greece's right to protect and defend its cultural patrimony;" and second, Macedonia would be admitted as the 'former Yugoslav Republic of Macedonia' until the name issue was resolved,[298] even though Macedonians deemed this "unwieldy"[299] name as derogatory and offensive.[300] The effects of forcing this name on the Republic of Macedonia requires that Macedonia has to sit in the "T" section at the UN, next to Thailand, because 'former' is not capitalized in the 'former Yugoslav Republic of Macedonia',[301] and because Greece objected to Macedonia sitting in the "M" section. This was the first time the UN ever admitted a country under a temporary name.[302] Further, Macedonia's admission was even deemed to consist of contradictory parts, as one section states that Macedonia fulfilled its obligation to be peace loving, while the next sentence says that the name dispute needs to be resolved in order to maintain peace.[303] Despite all of Macedonia's concessions, Greece still saw it unreasonable that Macedonia was rejecting other name solutions, such as when Macedonia rejected the name 'Slavomakedonija.'[304]

An EC opinion statement in 1993 even stated that "the name 'Macedonia' cannot therefore imply any territorial claim against another state" because of the constitutional concessions that Macedonia made.[305] The European countries during this time felt that diplomatic recognition of Macedonia would "help stabilize an ethnically mixed country in one of the most turbulent regions in the world."[306] As a matter of fact, out of the dozen EC members in October 1993, only Greece and France did not recognize the Macedonian government.[307]

In 1994, the US, along with several European countries, recognized Macedonia.[308] The US position was "confused and inconsistent" at first, as former Secretary of State James Baker stated, with President Clinton bowing to Greek pressure and not extending

---

[296] Floudas, Demetrius A., *Pardon? A Conflict for a Name?: Fyrom's Dispute with Greece Revisited*, 5.
[297] Bajalski, Borko, *Legal Aspects of Macedonia and Greece Name Dispute in Relation to UN Charter, the Interim Accord, and Macedonia's Integration to NATO/EU*, 8 (2009).
[298] Kofos, Evangelos, *Greece's Macedonian Adventure: The Controversy over FYROM's Independence and Recognition*, 6.
[299] http://news.bbc.co.uk/2/hi/europe/1737425.stm .
[300] Vangelov, Ognen, *The Greek Veto the Macedonian Identity*, 2.
[301] Siskind, Lawrence J., *It's Not All Greek to Them*, http://www.legaltimes.com April 2008.
[302] Floudas, Demetrius A., *Pardon? A Conflict for a Name?: Fyrom's Dispute with Greece Revisited*, 5.
[303] Bajalski, Borko, *Legal Aspects of Macedonia and Greece Name Dispute in Relation to UN Charter, the Interim Accord, and Macedonia's Integration to NATO/EU*, 7 (2009).
[304] Floudas, Demetrius A., *Pardon? A Conflict for a Name?: Fyrom's Dispute with Greece Revisited*, 5.
[305] Axt, Heinz-Jurgen et. al., *The Greek Macedonian Name Dispute -- Reconciliation through Europeanization?*, 12 (2006).
[306] Lewis, Paul, Europe *to Defy Greece on Ties to Macedonia*, http://select.nytimes.com/gst/abstract.html?res=F00616F83A5A0C718DDDAB0994DB494D81 Dec. 12th, 1993.
[307] *Greece Losing on Policy Over 'Macedonia'*, http://select.nytimes.com/gst/abstract.html?res=F00612FF3A580C758EDDA90994DB494D81 Oct. 26th, 1993.
[308] Floudas, Demetrius A., *Pardon? A Conflict for a Name?: Fyrom's Dispute with Greece Revisited*, 7.

full recognition to Macedonia.[309] Still, this was not enough to pacify the Greeks. Greece responded harshly to the recognitions by severing ties with Macedonia and imposing a blockade on goods coming from and going to Macedonia at Greece's port in Thessaloniki.[310] Even though all goods were not blocked, the Greek authorities were accused of "open[ing] and contaminat[ing] medicines before allowing them through to Macedonia, causing many preventable deaths."[311] US State Department officials actually blamed Clinton's refusal to establish "full diplomatic relations with Macedonia" as an action that legitimized the actions[312] of the new Greek Prime Minister, Andreas Papandreou, who eventually "succeeded in …rais[ing] a world outcry against Greece."[313]

Soon after the embargo the Europeans began questioning Greece's ability to be in the European Union and some even suggested removing Greece from the Union.[314] Then, on April 22, the European Commission brought an action under Article 225.2 of the EC Treaty, alleging that Greece had made improper use of Article 224 in order to justify the blockades of February 16th,[315] and "sought an interlocutory injunction that would suspend the measures taken by Greece."[316] The application for this injunction was eventually rejected because "the Commission failed to show the requisite urgency."[317]

Article 224 highlights when a country can take emergency measures, such as in the event of serious internal disturbances, war, the threat of war, or for maintaining peace and international security.[318] The EC argued that because the EC was an economic community, EC countries were not supposed to implement individual trade measures and could not deviate from a "common commercial policy based on uniform policies."[319] Greece argued that its "security [was] endangered, because Skopje's conduct constitute[d] a threat of war and the Greek people [were] so deeply disturbed that, without the economic sanctions imposed on [Macedonia], the public authorities would no longer be able to control the interior situation of the state."[320] In June of 1994 a decision was issued stating that this was a political dispute and not a legal one, and that the Commission had a lack of proof showing what harm Greece's actions had on the EC.[321]

Although the Macedonians posed no threat to Greece, Greece was still raging an ethnic war on its Macedonian minority. The Human Rights Watch reported in 1994 that

---

[309] Paquin, Jonathan, *Managing Controversy: U.S. Stability Seeking and the Birth of the Macedonian State*, 450 (2008).
[310] Floudas, Demetrius A., *Pardon? A Conflict for a Name?: Fyrom's Dispute with Greece Revisited*, 7.
[311] Warne, Leslie, *We Exist, Say Illawarra Macedonians*, http://www.greenleft.org.au/node/2031 Mar. 11th, 1992.
[312] Paquin, Jonathan, *Managing Controversy: U.S. Stability Seeking and the Birth of the Macedonian State*, 450 (2008).
[313] Kofos, Evangelos, *Greece's Macedonian Adventure: The Controversy over FYROM's Independence and Recognition*, 9.
[314] Floudas, Demetrius A., *Pardon? A Conflict for a Name?: Fyrom's Dispute with Greece Revisited*, 7.
[315] *Id.*
[316] Highet Keith et al., *European Community Law -- Greek--Slavo-Macedonian Conflict -- Embargoes.* 89 Am. J. Int'l L. 376, 377 (1994).
[317] *Id.*
[318] Floudas, Demetrius A., *Pardon? A Conflict for a Name?: Fyrom's Dispute with Greece Revisited*, 7.
[319] Highet Keith et al., *European Community Law -- Greek--Slavo-Macedonian Conflict -- Embargoes.* 89 Am. J. Int'l L. 376, 377 (1994).
[320] *Id.* at 376, 380.
[321] Floudas, Demetrius A., *Pardon? A Conflict for a Name?: Fyrom's Dispute with Greece Revisited*, 8.

Greek officials were still changing place names from Macedonian into Greek.[322] In November, a conference called 'Macedonia – Next Balkan Tragedy or Mode of Multi-culturalism' was held in London.[323] A University of Bradford professor, John Olcock, explained at the conference how the Macedonian ethnic identity still had managed to survive and persist despite even present "conditions of permanent usurpations and suppressions."[324]

In 1995, Greece had taken issue with supposed propaganda that was being spread in Macedonia, especially by Macedonians who had bumper stickers on their cars that suggested the entire geographical Macedonia was the Macedonians' historical homeland.[325] Macedonia responded that these were being spread by extremists and regular citizens who were upset with Greece.[326] Furthermore, Greece expressed objections to schoolbooks in Macedonia that showed maps of historical and geographical Macedonia.[327] Macedonia continually brought up the notion that an ethnic Macedonian minority resided in northern Greece; yet, Greece denied such existence.[328]

In the meantime, Macedonia insisted it had no territorial ambitions toward Greece; and even though it was the only country entirely located within geographical Macedonia, it was not claiming the rights to everything Macedonian.[329] Rather, Macedonia's sole objective was for Greece to stop having a monopoly over Macedonia and for Macedonia to be given self-determination in choosing its name.[330] Macedonia made these rather generous arguments despite being the first region to use the name 'Macedonia' officially,[331] and despite the fact that changing the country's name was against the people's will and would destabilize the country.[332]

Finally, the two nations came to a temporary agreement. In September of 1995, the foreign ministers of both countries signed an interim accord which ended Greece's sanctions and forced Macedonia to change its flag,[333] refrain from using symbols that were related to Greek heritage and culture, and again amend the constitution.[334] Macedonia gained Greece's recognition and a promise from Greece not to hinder Macedonia's efforts to obtain membership to international institutions and organizations.[335] Greece could only object to Macedonia joining such international organizations if it chose to seek admission under a name other than the 'former Yugoslav Republic of Macedonia.'[336] The EC then

---

[322] Human Rights Watch, *Denying Ethnic Identity: The Macedonians in Greece*, 17 (1994).
[323] Shea, John, *Macedonia and Greece: The Struggle to Define a New Nation*, 180.
[324] *Id.*
[325] Floudas, Demetrius A., *Pardon? A Conflict for a Name?: Fyrom's Dispute with Greece Revisited*, 6.
[326] *Id.*
[327] *Id.*
[328] *Id.*
[329] *Id.*
[330] *Id.*
[331] *Id.*
[332] *Id.*
[333] Tziampiris, Aristotle, *The Name Dispute in the Former Yugoslav Republic of Macedonia After the Signing of the Interim Accord*, 229.
[334] Floudas, Demetrius A., *Pardon? A Conflict for a Name?: Fyrom's Dispute with Greece Revisited*, 8.
[335] Tziampiris, Aristotle, *The Name Dispute in the Former Yugoslav Republic of Macedonia After the Signing of the Interim Accord*, 229.
[336] Axt, Heinz-Jurgen et. al., *The Greek Macedonian Name Dispute -- Reconciliation through Europeanization?*, 19 (2006).

dropped another legal action it had brought against Greece before the ruling was due.[337]

That same month, however, was extremely troubling for Macedonians in Greece, particularly for the ethnic Macedonian political party, Rainbow, established in Aegean Macedonia in 1994.[338] The political party opened up an office in Florin, with a sign that contained phrases in the Macedonian language.[339] The Greeks vehemently opposed the party, its office and the sign. The European Court of Human Rights, in a case against Greece that the Rainbow Party eventually won,[340] explained the events that ensued:

> Police officers removed the party's sign without giving any explanation to the applicants, who then put up a new sign. That evening, according to the applicants, while they were inside the party headquarters a crowd of people, among whom they apparently recognised the mayor, the deputy mayor and certain town councillors, gathered in front of the building to shout threats and insults at them, such as "traitors", "dogs", "death to the dogs of Skopje", "you're going to die", and "we'll burn everything". The crowd also allegedly demanded that the applicants hand over the sign.
>
> On 14 September 1995, at about 1.30 a.m. a number of people allegedly attacked the party headquarters, and, after breaking down the door, assaulted those inside and demanded that they hand over the sign, which the applicants did. Another group entered the premises at approximately 4 a.m., threw all the equipment and furniture out of the window and set it on fire. According to the applicants, throughout these events they made a number of telephone calls to the police station located some 500 metres from the party headquarters, but were apparently told that no officers were available to come out. The applicants submitted that the public prosecutor's office took no action against those involved in the incidents. However, criminal proceedings for inciting discord were brought against four members of the [Rainbow] party, including the second and third applicants, under Article 192 of the Criminal Code. The bill of indictment stated that "they had affixed to the party headquarters a sign on which, among other things, the word *vino-zito* (rainbow) was written in a Slavic language, and had thus sowed discord among the local inhabitants ...". The applicants were committed for trial.[341]

The discrimination and violence against ethnic Macedonians in Greece continued, despite Greece and Macedonia achieving a temporary agreement on the name issue.

Although many suggest the following years were relatively calm, much evidence exists to the contrary. Greece continued its confrontational stances against Macedonia by delaying the signing of the cooperation agreement between Macedonia and the EU; rejecting goods and certificates bearing the name 'Macedonia' coming from Macedonia; and not allowing Macedonia to participate in the Balkan Summit in Sofia over its objections to the name that it would use.[342] Macedonian Foreign Minister, Ljubomir Frckovski, responded with his own assertive attitude,[343] particularly by stating in July of 1996 that Macedonia was seeking recognition in the UN under its constitutional name.[344]

---

[337] Floudas, Demetrius A., *Pardon? A Conflict for a Name?: Fyrom's Dispute with Greece Revisited*, 8.

[338] *Case of Ouranio Toxo and Others. v. Greece*, Oct. 20th, 2005. European Court of Human Rights. http://www.pollitecon.com/html/treaties/Case_Of_Ouranio_Toxo_And_Others_v._Greece.html .

[339] *Id.*

[340] *Id.*

[341] *Id.*

[342] Tziampiris, Aristotle, *The Name Dispute in the Former Yugoslav Republic of Macedonia After the Signing of the Interim Accord*, 231.

[343] *Id.* at 230.

[344] *Id.* at 231.

Greece then accused Macedonia of acting in a way which conflicted with the spirit of the interim accord.[345]

In the meantime, Gligorov moved away from his original acceptance of 'Republic of Macedonia (Skopje)' and stated that Macedonia was ready to accept a double formula, in which Greece could call Macedonia whatever it wanted and the world would call Macedonia the 'Republic of Macedonia.'[346] Macedonian Minister of Foreign Affairs Blagoj Hadjinski also endorsed this view, in addition to stating that Greece could have a recognized region within its borders called 'Macedonia.'[347]

In 1996, Yugoslavia, which had disintegrated into a union of Serbia and Montenegro, established official diplomatic relations with Macedonia, squandering Macedonian fears of possible Serbian territorial claims against Macedonia. However, because of Greek pressure, Yugoslavia did not officially recognize Macedonia.[348] Still, the Greeks were upset because, in the agreement between Yugoslavia and Macedonia, Yugoslavia referred to Macedonia as the 'Republic of Macedonia.'[349]

In the summer of 1997, Macedonia finally sent an official request to Cyrus Vance, a diplomat for the UN, to be recognized under its constitutional name, the Republic of Macedonia.[350] Also during the summer, "the European Commission of Human Rights referred a case brought against the Hellenic Republic [Greece]" by seven ethnic Macedonians from Greece.[351] The seven plaintiffs, along with forty-nine others, were denied, by the Greek government and courts, to establish and register a nonprofit association called the 'Home of Macedonian Civilization' with the aim to promote the cultural and artistic heritage of its members in certain parts of Aegean Macedonia.[352] The first Greek court to hear this case, in 1990, found that, because some members were "engaged in promoting the idea that there is a Macedonian minority in Greece" (most notably through their participation in the Conference on Security and Cooperation in Europe), they could not obtain an application to register the group.[353]

The Macedonians appealed this decision, but the Greek appeals court dismissed their appeal.[354] The appeals court explained that the creation of such a cultural group was part of an overall effort by Macedonia to carve up part of Greece and gain access to the Aegean Sea.[355] The court also stated that "the purpose of using the term 'Macedonian' [in their association's name] is to dispute the Greek identity of Macedonia and its inhabitants" which "discerns an intention on the part of the founders to undermine Greece's territorial integrity."[356]

In 1994, the Macedonian plaintiffs then appealed this decision to the Greek Court

---

[345] *Id.*

[346] *Id.* at 234.

[347] *Id.*

[348] *Yugoslavia, Macedonia Set Up Diplomatic Ties*, <u>Milwaukee Journal Sentinel</u>, Apr. 9th, 1996: 49.

[349] *Id.*

[350] Kondonis, Haralambos, *Bilateral Relations Between Greece and the Former Yugoslav Republic of Macedonia*, 58.

[351] Sidropoulos and Others v. Greece. European Court of Human Rights.,10 Jul. 1998, (57/1997/841/1047) 1.

[352] *Id.* at 3.

[353] *Id.* at 4.

[354] *Id.*

[355] *Id.* at 7.

[356] *Id.*

of Cassation, which also denied their appeal.[357] Thus, this case was recommended to the European Court of Human Rights. The ECHR found "that the Greek courts' refusal to register the applicants' association amounts to an interference by the authorities with the applicants' exercise of their right to freedom of association[.]"[358] The Court also confronted the ethnic Macedonian minority issue:

> [A]ll the arguments put forward by the national courts and the Government against the association's founders were baseless, vague and unproved and did not correspond to the concept of "pressing social need". There was nothing in the case file to suggest that any of the applicants had wished to undermine Greece's territorial integrity, national security or public order. Mention of the consciousness of belonging to a minority and the preservation and development of a minority's culture could not be said to constitute a threat to "democratic society".
>
> [...]
>
> The "presence of some of the founders at the CSCE in Copenhagen could not be interpreted as an attack on national security, since the Greek Government themselves had, by signing all the relevant CSCE documents, recognised that citizens could take part in such proceedings. Nor had Mr Sidiropoulos in any way challenged the Greek identity of the Greek province of Macedonia; he had merely claimed that the Macedonian minority there was oppressed.[359]

The decision was a victory for the ethnic Macedonians in Greece, but also a boost to the Macedonian claim that Greece was in denial of the existence of ethnic Macedonians. It was viewed as support by the European community in the overarching 'Macedonian Question.'

In 1998 and 1999, the Kosovo crisis and war tested Macedonia's fragile democracy. Over 400,000 ethnic Albanian refugees flooded into Macedonia,[360] which is a number that was one-fifth of the total number of Macedonian citizens. This huge influx, combined with the war's other devastating effects of international trade disruption and the closing of transportation routes, cost Macedonia's tiny economy 1.5 billion dollars.[361] Furthermore, the Albanian separatist and terrorist movements in Kosovo and Presevo, regions in neighboring Serbia, heightened Macedonians' fears that Macedonia's Albanians would start fighting for independence.[362]

At the turn of the century, Macedonia became disturbed with statements by European officials.[363] When Johannes Swoboda, an Austrian member of the European Parliament, suggested that both Greece and Macedonia should find a mutually acceptable name in February of 2000,[364] Macedonia suspected that its European progress would depend on compromising over its name with Greece.[365] Many Macedonians then began

---

[357] *Id.* at 8.

[358] *Id.* at 17.

[359] *Id.* at 19-20.

[360] Tziampiris, Aristotle, *The Name Dispute in the Former Yugoslav Republic of Macedonia After the Signing of the Interim Accord*, 238.

[361] *Id.*

[362] *Id.* at 239.

[363] *Id.* at 236.

[364] *Id.*

[365] *Id.*

proclaiming that its provisional name status violated the UN Charter,[366] because Article 4 "strictly limits the conditions that can be imposed on membership," according to the ICJ.[367] President Boris Trajkovski of Macedonia also stated that Macedonia was the identity of the Macedonian nation, and thus Macedonia could not accept the name 'Upper Macedonia,'[368] which had been suggested at various points during the negotiations. A 2001 poll of Macedonians supported Trajkovski's remarks, as 90% of Macedonians said they were against a compromise with Greece over their name.[369] Even the ICG stated that Greece's positions were untenable and unsupported by a fair analysis of historical events.[370]

Yet, the ICG proposed solutions that both the Greeks and Macedonians could not accept. The ICG suggested that Macedonia should allow Greece to call it 'Upper Macedonia' in its dealings with Macedonia and how it refers to Macedonia internationally.[371] Further, the ICG suggested that Macedonia would not be allowed to object to the Greek commercial use of the name 'Macedonia' on certain goods.[372] While the ICG also stated that the EU, NATO and UN should use the 'Republic of Macedonia' in reference to Macedonia, the short name was suggested to be 'Republika Makedonija' and not 'Macedonia.'[373] Therefore, in the UN for example, Macedonia would be listed under and seated in the 'R' section, not the 'M' section.[374]

The Macedonian Academy of Arts and Sciences rejected these and other proposals for many reasons. The Academy stated that being called 'Upper Macedonia' would mean that people would be considered 'Upper Macedonians', not simply Macedonians.[375] This meant that the Macedonian identity along with the Macedonian name was being negotiated. [376] Furthermore, the Academy disagreed with the suggestion that their country's name could not be translated into English, but instead had to be referred to as 'Republika Makedonija', which utilizes the Latin alphabet, even though Macedonia does not use the Latin alphabet.[377] The Academy even objected to the notion that Macedonia should review the content of its school books while the same was not being requested of Greece.[378] Essentially, the Academy found the proposals to be unjust.

In the late winter of 2001, the name dispute was put on hold. Macedonia was dealt a blow from a different angle: "[e]thnic Albanian insurgents formed a paramilitary force [called] the National Liberation Army" and starting attacking Macedonians in the northwest areas of Macedonia.[379] Most of these Albanians were ex-fighters of the Kosovo

---

[366] *Id.*

[367] International Crisis Group, *Macedonia's Name: Why the Dispute Matters and How to Resolve It*, 17 (2001).

[368] Tziampiris, Aristotle, *The Name Dispute in the Former Yugoslav Republic of Macedonia After the Signing of the Interim Accord*, 240.

[369] *Id.*

[370] *Id.* at 243.

[371] *Id.* at 244.

[372] *Id.*

[373] *Id.*

[374] *Id.*

[375] *Id.* at 247.

[376] *Id.* at 244.

[377] *Id.* at 246.

[378] *Id.*

[379] Paquin, Jonathan, *Managing Controversy: U.S. Stability Seeking and the Birth of the Macedonian State*, 452 (2008).

Liberation Army[380] that terrorized both Serbian and Albanian populations in Kosovo before NATO bombed Serbia. They were Albanians with separatist ambitions.[381] This insurgency was not sudden; rather the Albanians had been planning it for many years prior:

> On 7 January 1998, the Kosovo Liberation Army [...] published its communique number 41, declaring that it was carrying the war into "Zone 2", in other words, the Republic of Macedonia. On 16 December 1997 a first bomb had gone off at the law courts in Gostivar, a [Macedonian] town with an Albanian majority. Two weeks later, the targets were the town halls of Kumanovo and Prilep, even though these two towns are not in the Albanian-speaking area.

> On 19 February 1998 there was a further escalation: in Gostivar a bomb blasted a butcher's shop belonging to an Albanian on good terms with the Macedonian authorities. "Wherever there are Albanians, you'll find the UÇK. It'll attack traitors first, in Macedonia as in Kosovo", Ibrahim Kelmendi, leader for Germany of the People's League of Kosovo (PLK - in Albanian Lëvizja Popullore e Kosovës, LPK), told us in Tirana on 14 April 1998.

> On 24 and 25 May the targets were the police stations in Gostivar and Skopje's Albanian quarter, Bit Pazar. Then on 21 July the Budapest-Athens train was struck near the Serbian-Macedonian border. On 28 September, the Macedonian security services arrested four Macedonian Albanians and issued arrest warrants against three others. Of these seven, four are students at the unofficial Albanian university in Tetovo.

> In the house used as offices for this university, which was set up illegally on 17 December 1994, a map of Greater Albania hangs on the wall. Apart from Albania and Kosovo, it includes the southern third of Montenegro, the western half of the Republic of Macedonia and part of the Greek provinces of Macedonia and Epirus, from Florina to the gulf of Arta. But the KLA has never carried its struggle into Montenegro or Greece. If the Republic of Macedonia has been its only victim so far, that is because it is the soft underbelly of the Albanian question and an easy target.[382]

Some Albanians claimed to be fighting for more language rights, but Macedonians still feared that their intentions were to carve apart Macedonia.[383] These desires are evident in one author's description of the beginning stages of the government's counterinsurgency tactics as described in *Time*:

> Having reinforced the town of Tetovo to stop the rebels swarming down and claiming it as the capital of the Albanian political entity they're trying to create in Macedonia, government forces are more likely now to settle in for siege, surrounding, harassing and containing the guerrillas while NATO forces along the Kosovo border stem the flow of men and weapons to the insurgents.[384]

NATO forces even engaged in brief armed skirmishes with these Albanians along the

---

[380] Karon, Tony, *Macedonia Contemplates a War of Attrition*, http://www.time.com/time/world/article/0,8599,103224,00.html Mar. 20th, 2001.
[381] *Id.*
[382] Chiclet, Christophe, *Macedonia Risks Falling Apart*, http://mondediplo.com/1999/01/13maced
[383] McNeil, Jr., Donald G., *NATO is Sending British Troops to Macedonia for Disarmament*, http://select.nytimes.com/gst/abstract.html?res=F60911FB3F5A0C758DDDA10894D9404482 . August 15th, 2001.
[384] Karon, Tony, *Macedonia Contemplates a War of Attrition*, http://www.time.com/time/world/article/0,8599,103224,00.html Mar. 20th, 2001.

border, as they were suspected of simply being remnants of the KLA.[385] For many years before this 2001 uprising, these Albanians were "considered by the CIA as a criminal gang of drug runners and terrorists[.]"[386]

In August, Macedonia signed a peace deal with its ethnic Albanian minority.[387] The deal called for 3,500 NATO troops to disarm the Albanian terrorists;[388] the establishment of Albanian as an official language where ethnic Albanians constituted at least one-fifth of the local population;[389] the government having to "finance Albanian-language higher education;"[390] the inclusion of over 1,000 Albanians in the Macedonian police force;[391] and rewording the Macedonian Constitution to remove certain references to ethnic Macedonians.[392] Most ethnic Macedonians viewed the peace deal as the West rewarding ethnic Albanians for a violent insurgency,[393] especially when Albanians were treated "relatively well" compared to the rest of the Balkan countries, and "even formed part of the [Macedonian] government coalition."[394] What especially irked most Macedonians is that the deal called for the amnesty of all Albanian terrorists and insurgents.[395] Furthermore, the agreement was only signed between ethnic Macedonian and ethnic Albanian politicians – there was nothing compelling the Albanians to, or guaranteeing that the Albanians would, put down their arms.[396]

The next couple years were relatively uneventful as Macedonia spent much time and resources recovering from the insurgency and rebuilding its government and economy. Then in November 2004, the US recognized Macedonia as the 'Republic of Macedonia'. The US did this because Macedonia was to hold a referendum on decentralization within a few days, and the US thought that by recognizing Macedonia under its constitutional name, the Macedonians would vote in favor of a "permanent, multi-ethnic, democratic state."[397]

---

[385] Marsden, Chris. *US Forces Conflict with KLA-backed Albanian Separatists in Macedonia*, http://www.wsws.org/articles/2001/mar2001/mac-m10.shtml . Mar. 10th, 2001.

[386] Marsden, Chris. *US Forces Conflict with KLA-backed Albanian Separatists in Macedonia*, http://www.wsws.org/articles/2001/mar2001/mac-m10.shtml . Mar. 10th, 2001.

[387] Fisher, Ian, *Macedonia Peace Signed, but Soon After, Artillery Booms*, http://select.nytimes.com/gst/abstract.html?res=F60E14F6355B0C778DDDA10894D9404482 . Aug. 13, 2001.

[388] *Id.*

[389] *Id.*

[390] *A Fragile Peace for Macedonia*, http://select.nytimes.com/gst/abstract.html?res=F30B12F7355B0C778DDDA10894D9404482 . Aug. 14th, 2001.

[391] Fisher, Ian, *Macedonia Peace Signed, but Soon After, Artillery Booms*, http://select.nytimes.com/gst/abstract.html?res=F60E14F6355B0C778DDDA10894D9404482 . Aug. 13, 2001.

[392] *Id.*

[393] *Id.*

[394] *A Fragile Peace for Macedonia.* http://select.nytimes.com/gst/abstract.html?res=F30B12F7355B0C778DDDA10894D9404482 . Aug. 14th, 2001.

[395] Fisher, Ian, *Macedonia Peace Signed, but Soon After, Artillery Booms*, http://select.nytimes.com/gst/abstract.html?res=F60E14F6355B0C778DDDA10894D9404482 . Aug. 13, 2001.

[396] *A Fragile Peace for Macedonia.* http://select.nytimes.com/gst/abstract.html?res=F30B12F7355B0C778DDDA10894D9404482 . Aug. 14th, 2001.

[397] Axt, Heinz-Jurgen et. al., *The Greek Macedonian Name Dispute -- Reconciliation through*

It might even be said that recognition was also a reward for Macedonia's military support and commitment in the Iraq war.[398] However, this US recognition once again heated matters between Macedonia and Greece.[399]

In April 2005 the UN mediator assigned to this dispute, Matthew Nimetz, offered a new name for Macedonia, the 'Republic of Macedonia-Skopje.'[400] "The suggestion uses the name of the capital in the same way that the Republic of Congo-Brazzaville incorporates the name of the city to distinguish it from the neighbouring Democratic Republic of Congo."[401] However, both Greece and Macedonia did not completely accept the name.[402] Macedonia was particularly concerned that, legally, the name would actually be 'Republika Makedonija – Skopje,' and not translated into English.[403] Furthermore, Greece's official country name did not include the term 'Macedonia'; thus, many Macedonians did not see a need for such a distinction.

In October, Nimetz put forward a proposal that Greece rejected.[404] The proposal offered 'Republic of Macedonia-Skopje' for bilateral relations between Greece and Macedonia; 'Republika Makedonija' for international organizations; and the 'Republic of Macedonia' with bilateral relations between Macedonia and other countries.[405] The essence of the solution is that neither Greece nor Macedonia would have sole claims to the name Macedonia.[406] However, Greece continued to insist that Macedonia use 'Republic of Macedonia-Skopje' for all dealings.

In 2007, when the Macedonian Srgjan Kerim was President of the UN General Assembly, he referred to Macedonia as the 'Republic of Macedonia', to which Greece immediately objected.[407] Greek ambassador John Mourikis wanted President Kerim to refer to Macedonia as the 'former Yugoslav Republic of Macedonia.'[408] President Kerim responded: "I am due to show full respect to the dignity of every single member state of the United Nations, including my own."[409] The Greek Foreign Ministry later stated that President Kerim "damaged … his … credibility as president of the General Assembly."[410] Soon, Greece then starting threatening that it would veto Macedonia's accession into NATO if a solution to the name dispute was not found.[411]

In June, Greece required its top diplomat to Macedonia, Dora Grosomanidou, to come back to Greece because of statements she made regarding Macedonia. Speaking to

---

Europeanization?, 27 (2006).
[398] *Id.*
[399] Apostolov, Mico, *The Macedonian Question -- Changes in Content Over Time*, vii (2006).
[400] *Greece Considers Macedonia Name*, http://news.bbc.co.uk/2/hi/europe/4425249.stm . Apr. 8th, 2005.
[401] *Id.*
[402] *Id.*
[403] *Macedonia: New Developments in Name Row With Greece*, www.rferl.org/content/article/1058423.html Apr. 13th, 2005.
[404] International Crisis Group, *Macedonia's Name: Breaking the Deadlock*, 5 (2009).
[405] *Id.*
[406] *Macedonia Accepts UN Name Proposals Despite Greek Rejection*, http://www.forbes.com/feeds/afx/2005/10/10/afx2268707.html . Oct. 10th, 2005.
[407] http://www.reuters.com/article/2007/09/25/us-un-assembly-macedonia-idUSN2539515020070925 September 25, 2007.
[408] *Id.*
[409] *Id.*
[410] *Id.*
[411] *Macedonia "No" to Trading Its Name*, http://www.balkaninsight.com/en/article/macedonia-no-to-trading-its-name . Nov. 5th, 2007.

the *Financial Times*, she stated: "Greece has to face the new reality, as the [f]ormer Yugoslav Republic of Macedonia has been recognized under its constitutional name (Macedonia) by more than half of the members of the UN[.]"[412] Greece wanted explanations,[413] because the comments were contradictory to Greece's official positions. Also in 2007, Canada recognized Macedonia as the 'Republic of Macedonia' for all bilateral relations between the two countries in September, much to the dismay of Greece.[414] "This decision doesn't please us," said Greek spokesman George Koumoustakos in a written statement, adding that "this decision will also displease hundreds of thousands of Greeks in Canada."[415]

On November 1st, Nimetz submitted a new set of proposals for a solution to the dispute.[416] This time, however, he did not suggest any new names, because he first wanted to make "suggestions in the form of a draft framework for their consideration as a basis for an honourable and fair solution."[417] As he remarked a month later, it was now "not an easy issue...[t]he position here [in Macedonia] and that in Greece are clear."[418] However, Macedonia rejected some of these talking points, because they would have required Macedonia to change its constitutional name for international usage.[419]

In 2008, Greece vetoed Macedonia's accession into NATO at the Bucharest Summit.[420] Prior to this veto, the West stepped up efforts to obtain a solution, especially after Greece's prime minister told the Greek Parliament in February that if no solution was found before the Bucharest Summit, Macedonia would not be invited into NATO.[421] NATO General Jaap de Hoop Sheffer visited Greece in order to dissuade the Greek officials from vetoing Macedonia's accession into NATO, stating that such a move would jeopardize regional security.[422] Further, the US sent Assistant Secretary of State for European Affairs Daniel Fried to Skopje to seek a Macedonian compromise.[423] In February, Nimetz also proposed five possible names: Democratic Republic of Macedonia, Constitutional Republic of Macedonia, Independent Republic of Macedonia, Republic of Upper Macedonia, and Northern Republic of Macedonia.[424] This appeared to have some effect on Macedonia's position. Speaking at the Bucharest Summit where Greece

---

[412] *Greek Diplomat Summoned Home Over Macedonia Comments*, http://www.forbes.com/feeds/afx/2007/07/06/afx3888877.html . Jun. 7th, 2007.

[413] *Id.*

[414] Petrakis, Maria, *Greece to Complain to Canada About 'Macedonia' Name Decision*, http://www.bloomberg.com/apps/news?pid=newsarchive&sid=aTd_F0R4xo98&refer=canada . Sep. 20th, 2007.

[415] *Id.*

[416] *U.N. Hands Greece and Macedonia Name Proposals*, http://uk.reuters.com/article/2007/11/01/uk-greece-macedonia-un-idUKN0146056820071101 . Nov. 1st, 2007.

[417] *Id.*

[418] *UN Envoy: Difficulty Between Macedonia, Greece over Name Issue*, http://mathaba.net/news/?x=573139 . Dec. 4th, 2007.

[419] *Macedonia "No" to Trading Its Name*, http://www.balkaninsight.com/en/article/macedonia-no-to-trading-its-name . Nov. 5th, 2007.

[420] Vankin, Sam, *Macedonians in Denial about the Name Issue Dispute With Greece*, June 5, 2009.

[421] *UMD Condemns Greek Threat to Veto Macedonia's NATO Membership*, http://umdiaspora.org/index.php?option=com_content&task=view&id=309&Itemid=1 . Feb. 24th, 2008.

[422] International Crisis Group, *Macedonia's Name: Breaking the Deadlock*, 6 (2009).

[423] *Id.*

[424] Seraphinoff, Michael, *Dimensions of the Greek-Macedonian Name Dispute*, 13 (2008).

eventually vetoed Macedonia's accession, Prime Minister Gruevski said that Macedonia would not submit to blackmail, and that NATO and European stability would be threatened due to a veto, but he did agree to 'Republic of Macedonia (Skopje)' for international organizations.[425] Greece rejected this since Greece wanted that name to be used in all relationships with all countries.[426]

After this veto, the Macedonia delegation walked out, with Foreign Minister Milososki stating: "Macedonia's bid for NATO membership was punished, not because of what we have done, but because of who we are."[427] President Crvenkovski stated that Macedonia "should not allow [itself] to be humiliated and to experience internal destabilization due to ill compromise."[428] The Greeks claimed this veto as a victory, with the Greek Ambassador stating: "NATO endorsed our position…[t]he requirement to solve the name issue is no longer a Greek position, it is now a NATO position and a multinational matter."[429] Thus, "Greece jeopardized the NATO Open Door Policy" with a veto of Macedonia's accession,[430] and then suggested that it was a NATO consensus which deprived Macedonia of accession.

In the summer of 2008, Greece filed a complaint to the Beijing Olympic Committee because it listed Macedonia under its constitutional name.[431] Macedonia's Deputy Prime Minister, Ivica Bocevski, replied that politics and bilateral disputes should not interfere with the spirit of the Olympics.[432] In November of 2008, Macedonia took Greece to the ICJ arguing that Greece should not block Macedonia into admission of international organizations under the provisional name the 'former Yugoslav Republic of Macedonia'[433] because doing so violates Article 11 of the Interim Accord signed between the two in 1995.[434] Greece responded by claiming Macedonia was not interested in a swift resolution, and that Macedonia violated the interim accord first by renaming its airport.[435] In the same month, "the Macedonian parliament passed a resolution calling on the government to define a strategy on the name dispute … that … must not 'endanger the Macedonian nation and its language, history, culture and identity.'"[436]

In 2009, the UN mediator proposed a plan to call Macedonia the 'Republic of North Macedonia,' in which Macedonia would be issued an invitation to join NATO and both countries could use the term Macedonian while refraining from making territorial against

---

[425] International Crisis Group, *Macedonia's Name: Breaking the Deadlock*, 6 (2009).
[426] *Id.*
[427] *Id.* at 7.
[428] http://www.canada.com/reginaleaderpost/news/story.html?id=e35b051a-688d-4c98-8062-aafb42a34f31 Sep. 25, 2008
[429] International Crisis Group, *Macedonia's Name: Breaking the Deadlock*, 7 (2009).
[430] Taleski, Dane, *Macedonia After the Greek Veto for Membership in NATO: Analysis of the Effects and the Situation*, 3 (2008).
[431] *Greek Olympic Committee Protests Over Macedonia Name Entry*, http://www.tehrantimes.com/index_View.asp?code=175024 .
[432] *Id.*
[433] International Crisis Group, *Macedonia's Name: Breaking the Deadlock*, 9 (2009).
[434] *"The former Yugoslav Republic of Macedonia institutes proceedings against Greece for a violation of Article 11 of the Interim Accord of 13 September 1995."* International Court of Justice, Press Release, November, 2008.
[435] International Crisis Group, *Macedonia's Name: Breaking the Deadlock*, 9 (2009).
[436] Kosanic, Zoran, *Obstacles to FYROM's Membership of NATO: A Tougher Agenda Than Expected*, 3 (2009).

one another.[437] Macedonia and Greece both rejected this proposal.[438] Macedonian Prime Minister Gruevski iterated in July that "one name for communication with Greece, while [allowing] the constitutional name to be valid for all other countries" is Macedonia's position.[439]

Also in early 2009, Macedonian Ambassador Kire Ilioski expressed frustration because Macedonia fulfilled all necessary criteria for NATO membership and still could not get in because of the name dispute.[440] In September of 2009, the UN Committee on the Elimination of Racial Discrimination then recommended that Greece "adopt measures to ensure the effective enjoyment by persons belonging to every community or group of their right to freedom of association and of their cultural rights, including the use of mother languages."[441]

Today, the dispute appears to be at a standstill. Currently, over two-thirds of UN countries recognize Macedonia as the 'Republic of Macedonia' for bilateral relations.[442] Most of Macedonia's demands have intensified and now revolve around one common theme: identity. For example, Prime Minister Nikola Gruevski sent a letter to Nimetz asking that the Greek Orthodox Church's refusal to recognize the Macedonian Orthodox Church be included in the negotiations.[443] Macedonians' neighbors refuse to recognize the legitimacy of the Macedonian church, even though history has shown that the Macedonian Church has existed for many years. This is important for Macedonia because her neighboring countries' Orthodox Churches also consistently promote the ideas of Greater Serbia, Bulgaria or Greece in Macedonia,[444] which is a constant threat to the nation.

Moreover, Macedonia has responded with anger and determination due to the Greek veto. Greece is actively denying Macedonia entry into NATO; yet, as of January 2010, Macedonia has more troops in Afghanistan than Greece,[445] itself a NATO member, which Macedonia believes demonstrates its will to be committed to NATO ideals and principles.[446] Macedonia actually has more troops per capita than any other country in the mission.[447] US President Obama keeps asking more troops from Macedonia, which Macedonia has granted;[448] yet, NATO still refuses to reward Macedonia, upsetting

---

[437] Vankin, Sam, *The Republic of North Macedonia and Palestine: Obama Loses Patience With Bush Allies*, June 3, 2009.

[438] *Id*.

[439] *Macedonia's Gruevski Backs double formula in name dispute*, July 22, 2009, http://www.setimes.com/cocoon/setimes/xhtml/en_GB/newsbriefs/setimes/newsbriefs/2009/07/22/nb-01

[440] *Assessing the Security Implications of Balkan Integration*, 8 (2009).

[441] International Convention on the Elimination of All Forms of Racial Discrimination. *Concluding observations of the Committee on the Elimination of Racial Discrimination: Greece*, September, 2009: 4.

[442] *Macedonia "No" to Trading Its Name*. http://www.balkaninsight.com/en/article/macedonia-no-to-trading-its-name . Nov. 5th, 2007.

[443] http://micnews.com.mk/node/14749 *Gruevski asks of Nimetz resolution of church issue as well*, August 13, 2008.

[444] Shea, John, *Macedonia and Greece: The Struggle to Define a New Nation*, 175.

[445] Greece had 15 troops while Macedonia had 165. See *Greece Must Reform Politically as Well as Economically*. http://greatersurbiton.wordpress.com/2010/02/28/greece-must-reform-politically-as-well-as-economically/ . Feb. 28th, 2010.

[446] McNamara, Sally, *It is Past Time for Macedonia to Join NATO*, 1 (2010).

[447] McNamara, Sally and Morgan L. Roach, *The Obama Administration Must Push for Macedonia's Accession to NATO at the Lisbon Summit*, The Heritage Foundation. Web Memo No. 3037, 2 (2010).

[448] *Id*.

Macedonians everywhere. Further, minority rights for Macedonians (among others) in Greece are now a crucial aspect of the negotiations, along with the return of property to Macedonians who were either expelled or left voluntarily.[449]

Currently, Macedonia and Greece are awaiting the ICJ's decision on Macedonia's suit against Greece. The decision, whether it comes out for Macedonia or for Greece, will likely have no impact on either country's positions.

---

[449] International Crisis Group, *Macedonia's Name: Breaking the Deadlock*, 7 (2009).

B. Why the Negotiations have Failed

There are many reasons why the negotiations between Macedonia and Greece have failed to produce a solution. Many argue that the reason for this is that the issue is a non-negotiable issue for the Macedonians, which is likely to be the truth. However, there are also specific reasons why the negotiations in particular have not worked, mostly due to bad faith on the part of Greece.

1. Greece's denial of the ethnic Macedonian identity

All our problems started when the Greeks came ... They wouldn't even let me speak to my mother in Macedonian because it was a 'dirty language'. I have vivid memories of my grandmother being made to learn Greek at night school when she was in her late 80s.[450]

As demonstrated in Part A, the dispute between Macedonia and Greece is much more than a name dispute. In actuality, rejecting Macedonia's name has been the central political weapon Greece has used to eradicate the ethnic Macedonian identity. By shifting the dispute from the core issue (the Macedonian identity) to a branch of the core issue (the name of Macedonia), Greece has managed to mask the grueling moral and legal dimensions of its history and viewpoints regarding the Macedonian Question. Further, by framing the issue as being about one country trying to steal another country's historical rights to a name, Greece has succeeded in portraying the dispute as one of political stubbornness. The international policy makers, removed from the history and roots of the Macedonian questions, are thus left to believe that the two countries' political maneuvers is what has resulted in such a long and drawn out negotiation process.

But regardless of attempts to mask the underlying issue, the leading cause of the failed negotiations and a resolution to the name hinges on two crucial points. First, Greece refuses to admit that an ethnic Macedonian people exist separate from any other ethnic group.[451] Second, Greece denies that people who consider, and have considered, themselves ethnic Macedonians live within Greece's borders, which is still a major source of contention as of this writing.[452] As the Macedonians understand it, and as Loring Danforth described, these Greek policies amount to a "symbolic ethnic cleansing that could lead to ... active ethnic cleansing."[453] The Macedonians ferociously claim that their existence hangs in the balance.

Because Greece denies the existence of a separate Macedonian identity, and therefore argues that the land it annexed in 1913 had always been part of Greek history and culture, many Greeks argue that today's 'fyromians' have no rights to Greek heritage.[454]

---

[450] Smith, Helena, *Bittersweet Return for Greek Civil War's Lost Victims: Greece is Allowing Ethnic Macedonians Exiled in the 1940s to Revisit Their Homes for the First Time*, http://www.guardian.co.uk/world/2003/oct/17/greece . Oct. 17, 2003. Quote by Maria Buntevska.

[451] Engstrom, Jenny, *The Power of Perception: The Impact of the Macedonian Question on Inter-ethnic Relations in the Republic of Macedonia*, 1 The Global Review of Ethnopolitics 3, 2002: 9.

[452] Gay McDougall Mission to Greece, *Promotion and Protection of All Human Rights, Civil, Political, Economic, Social and Cultural Rights, Including the Right to Development*, 13 (2009).

[453] Shea, John, *Macedonia and Greece: The Struggle to Define a New Nation*, 181.

[454] Vankin, Sam, *Gruevski's Macedonia, Greece, and Alexander the Great, History's Forgotten Madman*,

Macedonia, however, asserts that there is such a thing as a Macedonian language, people and identity, as evidence by the fact that 70% of ethnic Macedonians in Macedonia declare they identify as such, and that well over a million people outside of Macedonia identify as such.[455] Still, Greece has persistently denied that a separate ethnic Macedonian people exist. For example, in the early 1900s, Greece teamed up with Bulgaria and Serbia in denying the existence of a Macedonian national identity[456] in order to serve their own irredentist desires. Greece wavered back and forth from calling the Macedonians "Slavophone Greeks and Bulgarians"; Bulgarians claimed Macedonia and Macedonians as their own; and Serbs considered them 'South Serbians'.[457] Many of these claims persist.

However, among the Greeks, confusion and inconsistency is commonplace and widespread as to what they believe should be the true identity of these Macedonians. Aside from officially spewing the degrading term 'Skopjians', different Greeks refer to Macedonians as Slavs, Bulgarians, southern Serbs, Slavophone Greeks, fyromians, or as an unclassified fusion of Turks, Roma, and Slavs. A good portion even consider the Macedonians to be confused Greeks. Therefore, it is not surprising that the ICG concluded that Macedonia had no margin to concede in matters of identity to Greece, Bulgaria, or Serbia.[458] Despite this acknowledgment, the political nature of the dispute and the complicated history of the Macedonian Question has placed the Macedonians in a position where they have to defend, explain, and justify their identity.

In this section, I will first show that Macedonians are not Bulgarians, Serbs, Slavs or Greeks. Then I will demonstrate that there is a separate ethnic Macedonian identity and that there are people within Greece who are ethnic Macedonians. After that, I briefly discuss the nation and identity of Greece and the Greeks. I will conclude by demonstrating how Greece's denial of the Macedonian identity affects the negotiations, and sequentially, the existence of Macedonia.[459]

Not Bulgarians

As mentioned earlier, one of the more popular and disrespectful terms hurled at the ethnic Macedonians is that they are really Bulgarians. This term is not disrespectful because the Macedonians have something against the ethnic Bulgarians. Rather, the Macedonians simply are opposed to being called something that they are not. When the Bulgarians label a Macedonian 'Bulgarian,' it may not be intended to degrade the Macedonians. Bulgarians label Macedonians as such because they either genuinely believe that Macedonians are Bulgarian, or because they believe Macedonia belongs to Bulgaria. As one Bulgarian diplomat stated, "[t]here is no Macedonia. It is Western Bulgaria."[460] For most Macedonians, however, these accusations are associated with great pain and

---

(2009).

[455] Marinov, Tchavdar, *We, the Macedonians: The Paths of Macedonian Supra-Nationalism (1878-1912)*, in *We, the People: Politics of National Peculiarity in Southeastern Europe* by Diana Mishkova, 131 (2009).

[456] International Crisis Group, *Macedonia's Name: Breaking the Deadlock*, 2 (2009).

[457] International Crisis Group, *Macedonia's Name: Why the Dispute Matters and How to Resolve It*, 11 (2001).

[458] Tziampiris, Aristotle, *The Name Dispute in the Former Yugoslav Republic of Macedonia After the Signing of the Interim Accord*, 243.

[459] Engstrom, Jenny, *The Power of Perception: The Impact of the Macedonian Question on Inter-ethnic Relations in the Republic of Macedonia*, 1 The Global Review of Ethnopolitics 3, 2002: 9.

[460] Kaplan, Robert D., *Balkan Ghosts: A Journey Throughout History*, 59 (1993).

haunting memories, as they whirl up fears of their existence being in jeopardy and their territory being pursued. As one Macedonian priest painfully recalled of the Balkan wars during the early 1900s, when a rifle was pointed at his chest, a Bulgarian ordered, "[b]ecome a Bulgarian, or I'll kill you."[461]

Throughout history, Macedonians have occasionally associated with Bulgaria, whether it was through the Bulgarian Church in the 1800s because Macedonians could not have their own church, or because of political opportunities to reunite Macedonia and better their lives, or because of ethnic assimilation of the Macedonians by Bulgaria. William B. King explained the reason for Macedonians doing so during World War II:

> When the mass exchange of populations took place in the Balkans following the first World war, many Slavs chose to remain in Greece. There, during the recent Bulgar occupation on behalf of the Germans, many Greek Slavs announced themselves as Bulgarian nationals and co-operated with the invaders. This may have saved them from the authorities of the program to 'Bulgarianize' all Macedonia, which is split among Greece, Bulgaria and Yugoslavia; but it did not endear them to their Greek neighbors. As partisan movements grew throughout the Balkans, many men of Slavic families, even some of those who had collaborated at first, fled to the woods to fight. Some joined Tito's partisans, and some the Elas. Thus, regardless of is justification, these people earned themselves further enmity of the present powers in Greece, who count as enemies all who participated in leftist movements. [...] The minister for Macedonia with the central Yugoslav government is Emanuel Cuckov, who is so anxious for Macedonian autonomy that he co-operated with the Bulgars in the early part of the occupation, in an effort to promote the scheme through them. He [...] soon saw the program could not succeed through the Bulgars and turned to the federation scheme of Tito's liberation movement.[462]

Shortly later, in the 1960s and 1970s, Bulgaria gave Macedonians economic incentives to join their alliance:

> Bulgaria has gone so far in its nonrecognition of Macedonia that Macedonians traveling through Bulgaria are treated as Bulgarians – or even better. They are offered jobs, scholarships and special discounts in tourist shops across the border. 'Our citizens are constantly being offered employment in Bulgaria at far better pay than Bulgarians,' Macedonian writer Vlada Miletic said. 'They are invited to study in Bulgaria on scholarships twice as big as those allotted Bulgarian students.'[463]

Thus, Macedonians 'became Bulgarian' hoping that it would help free and unite the Macedonian people; or at least they did so to attain pathways that could better their lives.

But the Macedonians and Bulgarians are, and have always been, distinct people. An article in the *New York Times* from 1884 demonstrates a sharp contrast between the social structure of the Bulgarians and Macedonians, during the time:

> The Bulgarian before his liberation was little more than a beast of burden, but he had no special vices; the Macedonian, on the contrary, in addition to proclivities to filth, is inclined to be a thief, a highwayman, and even an assassin, or, if physically incapable of crime needing physical assertion, is an accomplice after the fact: in other words, one half of the Macedonians are disposed to kill and rob and the other half to act as receivers of stolen

---

[461] Agnew, John, *No Borders, No Nations: Making Greece in Macedonia*, 97 Annals of the Association of American Geographers 2, 2007: 405.

[462] King, William B., *Trouble is Brewing in the Balkans*, The Milwaukee Journal, Jul. 29, 1945: 46.

[463] Djuric, Nesho, *Macedonia Remains Balkan Sore Spot*, Beaver County Times. Aug. 8th, 1972: 5.

booty.[464]

Certainly, the passage emphasizes the characteristics of the Macedonians during a time when Macedonians were rebelling against Ottoman oppression and the unjust campaign by their neighbors to infiltrate Macedonia and conquer it. Further, this passage does not distinguish Macedonians from Bulgarians on ancestral grounds. Still, the author distinguished between the Bulgarians and Macedonians on political, social and geographic grounds, which were more accepted ways of distinguishing groups of people than ancestral affinity. Further, the author did not claim these people were the Bulgarians of Macedonia.

Yet, ethnicity in the Balkans was really a nonexistent concept before the 19th century. Being Bulgarian in the 1800s meant that you supported the Bulgarian Exarchate.[465] Calling yourself a Bulgarian had everything to do with linguistics and religion, and nothing to do with ethnic affiliation.[466] But even though speakers of the Macedonian language "gravitated toward the Bulgarian church after its establishment in 1870, they referred to themselves as Macedonians."[467] This shows that Macedonians desired to affiliate with a Macedonian church and a Macedonian establishment rather than a Bulgarian one. Andrew Rossos highlights the sharp divide between Macedonians and Bulgarians in the 1860s:

> Educated Macedonians embraced the name of their land as a national name and symbol and rose in defense of Macedonian interests. They argued— and the Bulgarian press condemned them—that "a Bulgarian and a Bulgarian language was one thing and a Macedonian and a Macedonian language something else." They insisted that it was necessary "to protect the Macedonian youth," who "should be taught and should develop exclusively in the Macedonian speech." Indeed, some of these "Makedonisti," as the Bulgarian press called them, went much further. They claimed to be the "purest Slavs" and "descendants of the ancient Macedonians" of Philip and Alexander.[468]

Other reports from the late 1800s demonstrate that Macedonians "insisted that they were not Bulgarian, wanted their own, separate church, and resisted the 'east' Bulgarian language in their literature."[469] Moreover, there is further evidence to show that, even if the Bulgarians thought Macedonians were Bulgarian, there were factions of Macedonians who desired no political affiliation with Bulgaria, and rather wanted to be free of the Bulgarian grip. This is partly evidenced in an 1886 article in *The Philadelphia Record*: "A Macedonian Voivoide [soldier] . . . admitted that he was the leader of a band of Macedonians . . .organized to act against the [Bulgarian] Government."[470] The passage does not state whether these were Macedonians in the geographic sense, or Macedonians in the ethnic sense; but it does highlight tensions between Macedonians and Bulgaria.

The validity of these reports is confirmed by several Rules of the Macedonian Rebel Committee:

---

[464] *"The Turks in Macedonia; Reported Atrocities and the Basis they Have," * New York Times, December 25, 1884.
[465] Mazower, Mark, *Salonica: City of Ghosts, Christians, Muslims, and Jews, 1430-1950*, 248 (2000).
[466] *Id.*
[467] Glenny, Misha, *The Balkans: Nationalism, War and The Great Power, 1804 – 1999*, 157 (2000).
[468] Rossos, Andrew, *Macedonia and the Macedonians*, 85 (2008).
[469] *Id.* at 86.
[470] *Bulgarian Elections*, The Philadelphia Record. October 12, 1886: 1.

200. The Holy Exarchate of Bulgaria, with His Holiness at its head, carries out a policy which is more than odd, since, on the pretext that it is caring for the Macedonians who remain under the immediate authority of the Turks, it maintains close relations with the Turkish government in Constantinople and is great friends with it; it believes that, by pleasing the Turks, it will gain some influence over them to send spiritual leaders (bishops) into Macedonia who will protect the Macedonian population from its oppressors. What a destiny for Macedonia! The Macedonian Rebel Committee does not approve of such an awkward, policy which breaks up the concentrated forces of the people and ties Macedonia's hands for her liberation

201. The Macedonian Rebel Committee invites the clergy in Macedonia not to carry out the Exarchate's orders in the country but to join the Macedonian people in revolt until the liberation, and later the Church question in Macedonia will also be settled.

202. The Macedonian Rebel Committee will send a deputy to His Holiness, Exarch Joseph l, in Constantinople to ask him not to hinder the Macedonian Uprising if he does not wish to be included within the ranks of the traitors.

203. His Grace, the Reverend Meletij of Sofia, [Bulagaria], who, playing the role of a helper to our Macedonian Uprising, has caused a lot of damage to our cause, will also be asked to give up his intentions, and since he does not help the Uprising, not to harm it.

205. The Macedonian Rebel Committee, by adopting these rules, that is, this Constitution, decrees that, from now on the Sofia Central Committee has no more responsibilities towards the Macedonian Uprising.

206. All the orders of the Sofia Central Committee are repealed and the Uprising will be guided by the Macedonian Rebel Committee, which is in Macedonia.[471]

Furthermore, Rule 186 stated that "[t]he Macedonian Rebel Committee will also inform the government of the Principality of Bulgaria that the Macedonians will have no dealings with the Principality other than those of fraternal aid from our Slav brothers."[472] This revealing rule demonstrates that, although the Macedonians viewed the Bulgarians as 'Slav brothers' of the Macedonians, they did not view themselves as Bulgarians.

But some Bulgarians suggest that Hristo Silijanov, an active member in the early 20th century Macedonian uprising, claimed the IMRO was really Bulgarian. Silijanov suggested in his "The Liberation Movement – The Ilinden Uprising" that the founders of IMRO believed the organization was Bulgarian.[473] As John Shea explains:

However, given the use of the label 'Bulgarian' at the time, it should probably not be understood with its modern meaning. It may be synonymous with 'every Slav with Bulgarian Church affiliation,' or it may simply reflect the fact that the conspirators used the Bulgarian constitution as their first model and gradually introduced changes. I suggest this because clearly some of the original conspirators born in Macedonia of parents born in Macedonia; they used the Macedonian name for their organization; they planned for Macedonian autonomy; they spoke of 'Macedonia for the Macedonians'; they said they wanted a Switzerland of the Balkans, implying acceptance of different ethnic/language groups.[474]

---

[471] *Rules of the Macedonian Rebel Committee,*
http://documents-mk.blogspot.com/2009/12/blog-post_30.html . Last accessed February 27, 2011.
[472] *Id.*
[473] Shea, John, *Macedonia and Greece: The Struggle to Define a New Nation*, 168.
[474] Shea, John, *Macedonia and Greece: The Struggle to Define a New Nation*, 168.

Thus, even though the Macedonians did not have their own formal state or church, they believed they were not Bulgarians.

One of Bulgaria's attempts to claim Macedonians as their own is by stating that the Macedonian language is really a dialect of Bulgarian. However, "the Turko-Tatar Bulgars settled the Eastern Balkans 150 years after Slav tribes and took the Slavic language from them."[475] So, in a way, it could be said that Bulgarians really speak a dialect of Macedonian, as Macedonians spoke modern-Macedonian before Bulgarians spoke modern Bulgarian. The only difference is that, because of its political and economic might, Bulgaria was able to institutionalize and formalize its language well before Macedonia.

Yet, maybe the most damaging evidence to the claim comes from the Bulgarian government itself in the 1940s. In 1946, "the inhabitants of Pirin Macedonia were openly encouraged to register themselves with the Bulgarian Ministry of Interior—not as Bulgars, but as Macedonians. [...] [A]ccording to State Department reports, up to 70 percent of the inhabitants of Pirin Macedonia declared themselves to be Macedonian."[476] Thus, the evidence exists to refute any claims that Macedonians are really just Bulgarians.

Not Greeks

A 1902 *New York Times* article titled "Greeks Betrays Macedonians"[477] in itself may be enough to show that Greeks and Macedonians are two different peoples. But there is much more evidence to confirm this. Rule 39 of the Macedonian Rebel Committee refers to the "Grecomaniacs ... hav[ing] a secret agreement with the Turks to sow confusion among the [Macedonian] population."[478] And during the Greek Civil War of the 1940s, Macedonian Lazo Ristovski wrote to the leaders of the Greek Communist Party:

> Do they or don't they have the right, . . . in accordance with the eight points of the Atlantic Charter on the self-determination of nations, to demand, together with the other two parts under Serbia and Bulgaria, to establish their own Slavmacedonian people's republic?! The Slavmacedonians justly ask: Why do they not permit us to develop fully our national culture and to realize our national ideals . . . ?! We are not Greeks, but a Slavmacedonian nation, with different ideals. How could we remain in Greece, content solely with equality? How could this be reconciled with the basic principles on the self determination of nations?[479]

Today, it has been said that about two-thirds of the 53,000 people in Florina (in Aegean Macedonia) are ethnic Macedonians.[480] One of these Macedonians, who belongs to a human rights group, stated that he was Macedonian and different from other Greek citizens.[481] Another Macedonian in Greece stated: "I am a Greek citizen...but I am a

---

[475] Schteppan, Hans L., *Comedy: Greek By Name*. http://maknews.com/html/articles/stefov/stefov121.html . February, 2008.

[476] Van Meter, David C., *The Macedonian Question and the Guerrilla War in Northern Greece on the Eve of the Truman Doctrine*, Journal of the Hellenic Diaspora, 81.

[477] *Greeks Betray Macedonians*, The New York Times, March 31, 1902: 9.

[478] *Rules of the Macedonian Rebel Committee,* Rule 194 http://documents-mk.blogspot.com/2009/12/blog-post_30.html . Last accessed February 27, 2011.

[479] Rossos, Andrew, *Incompatible Allies: Greek Communism and Macedonian Nationalism in the Civil War in Greece, 1943-1949*, 69 The Journal of Modern History 1, 1997: 50.

[480] Human Rights Watch, *Denying Ethnic Identity: The Macedonians in Greece*, 14 (1994).

[481] *Id.*

Macedonian when talking about my village, my language and my identity."[482] It is apparent that a Macedonian ethnicity exists separate and distinct from a Greek ethnicity.

Not Serbs

The claim that ethnic Macedonians are actually southern Serbs is also easily refuted. According to an article from 1885 in the *Nelson Evening Mail*, "King Milan [of Serbia] has declared that if the Macedonians rose in revolt he must act with them, or otherwise he would be disposed."[483] Certainly, this does not say that Macedonians are not Serbs. However, King Milan also did not say if 'Macedonia' rose in revolt, nor if 'Serbs in Macedonia' rose in revolt, that he would act. He specifically stated 'Macedonians.' Further, he did not refer to people within his kingdom with geographic qualifiers; he referred to them as Serbs.

Further evidence can be found throughout history. Rule 136 of the Macedonian Rebel Committee of 1878 stated that 'Macedonians in Serbia' could join the Macedonian uprising, as long as they could find weapons.[484] Then, writing in the early 1900s, John Reed said, "[t]he Serbs gave the unhappy Macedonians 24 hours to renounce their nationality and pronounce themselves Serbs…"[485] Even though some Serbs still believe Macedonians are really Serbs, this claim is no longer with any merit. "Rightly or wrongly, these [people][486] […] consider themselves Macedonians, not Serbs, and both the Greeks and the Serbs must come to term with this fact."[487]

Not Bulgarians or Serbs

One can even find evidence for the Macedonian identity in the American court system. The Supreme Court of the US state of Indiana, writing in 1929, mentioned that an appellate of a previous case was Macedonian,[488] while mentioning other people as Bulgarian and even others as Serbian.[489]

We find these distinctions between Serbs, Bulgarians and Macedonians much earlier. In the late 1800s, William Gladstone, who was England's Prime Minister three times, stated: "… [n]ext to the Ottoman government nothing can be more deplorable and blameworthy than jealousies between Greek and Slav and plans by the states already existing for appropriating other territory. Why not Macedonia for the Macedonians as well as Bulgaria for the Bulgarians and Serbia for the Serbians." [490] As Metropolitan Mikhail puts it today: "I am a real Macedonian. I know what I am. I am a sparrow, not a Bulgarian,

[482] Gay McDougall Mission to Greece, *Promotion and Protection of All Human Rights, Civil, Political, Economic, Social and Cultural Rights, Including the Right to Development*, 14 (2009).

[483] *The Roumelian Revolt*, Nelson Evening Mail, October 20, 1885: 3.

[484] *Rules of the Macedonian Rebel Committee*, http://documents-mk.blogspot.com/2009/12/blog-post_30.html . Last accessed February 27, 2011.

[485] Kaplan, Robert D., *Balkan Ghosts: A Journey Throughout History*, 64 (1993).

[486] Kaplan uses the term 'Slavs'.

[487] *Id.* at 68.

[488] Kostoff v. Meyer-Keiser Bank,167 N.E. 527, 530. 1929.

[489] Kostoff v. Meyer-Keiser Bank,167 N.E. 527, 528. 1929.

[490] *The Macedonian-Greek Conflict: The Age Long Conflict between the Greeks and the Macedonians*, http://www.historyofmacedonia.org/MacedonianGreekConflict/conflict.html

not an eagle of Serbia."[491]

Not Greeks nor Bulgarians

It is official policy of Greece and Bulgaria to deny the Macedonian ethnicity.[492] Thus, Macedonians have to "tirelessly point to a 'long history' to …legitimize them as an ('ethnic') nation."[493] Fortunately, this evidence is easy to find. Evidence exists stating that Macedonians were a group of Christians separate from the Greeks and Bulgarians. In 1875, Gjorgi Pulevski wrote: "I am not Bulgarian, nor Greek, nor Tzintzar, I am pure Macedonian as were Philip and Alexander the Macedonian and Aristotle [the] Philosopher."[494] A *New York Times* article from 1890 highlights, by referring to the Macedonians as Christians, suggests that they used the term in a meaning other than geographical: "The Christians, a herd of Greeks, Bulgarians, and Macedonians, with the most villainous faces, morals, and manners imaginable, have to be ruled with a tight hand to be kept from strangling one another."[495]

A Russian official of the early 1900s also spoke of the Macedonians being separate from the Greeks and Bulgarians:

> In August–September 1907, M. Petraiev, a Russian consular official and keen Balkan observer, accompanied Hilmi Pasha, inspector general for Macedonia, and an Austro-Hungarian representative on a tour of Macedonia. Afterward, he reported to his Ministry of Foreign Affairs: "In the Kastoria kaza, delegations from the villages came to see us and declared that they wanted neither Greek nor Bulgarian teachers and priests; rather, they insisted that they be Macedonians. When questioned about their nationality, they replied that they are Macedonians. These declarations, which are far from being isolated, demonstrate that the Christian population of Macedonia is fed-up with the oppression of the various propagandas, and that in them is beginning to awaken a national consciousness different from those being imposed on them from the outside."[496]

Present day authors acknowledge this fact also. It has been demonstrated that "[m]ost Slav Christian peasants in the Salonica countryside [(a region in Aegean Macedonia)] did not count themselves as either Greeks of Bulgarians in the late 1800s and early 1900s."[497] One author even explained how groups of Greeks, Bulgarians, and Macedonians would fight amongst each other to gain support from other Christians.[498]

Not Slavs

From a letter to the editor in the *New York Times* by Vladimir Tsanoff in 1903, we learn much about Macedonians: "You slandered the Macedonians by calling them 'descendants of degenerate Slav tribes and the vagabond followers of the early Christian Crusades . . . Such a statement might apply to those in Macedonia who speak the Greek

---

[491] Kaplan, Robert D., *Balkan Ghosts: A Journey Throughout History*, 68 (1993).

[492] Wieland, Carsten, *One Macedonia with Three Faces: Domestic Debates and Nation Concept*, 6.

[493] Wieland, Carsten, *One Macedonia with Three Faces: Domestic Debates and Nation Concept*, 6.

[494] *The Macedonian-Greek Conflict: The Age Long Conflict between the Greeks and the Macedonians*, http://www.historyofmacedonia.org/MacedonianGreekConflict/conflict.html

[495] *Article 10*, New York Times, June 8, 1890: 18.

[496] Rossos, Andrew, *Macedonia and the Macedonians*, 89 (2008).

[497] Mazower, Mark, *Salonica: City of Ghosts, Christians, Muslims, and Jews, 1430-1950*, 239 (2004).

[498] Kechriotis, Vangelis, *Greek-Orthodox, Greek-Ottomans, or Just Greeks? Theories of Ethnic Coexistence on the Eve of the Fall of the Ottoman Empire*, 2.

language, but there are only a very few such thousand in Macedonia."[499] These words emphasize that Macedonians are not simply 'just Slavs' without any other identifying cultural or ancestral features.

Nothing but Macedonians

The Macedonians have been around for a few millennia. However, prior to the 1800s, there is not much information about the Macedonian ethnic identity or other Balkan peoples' identity because all of the Orthodox people in the Ottoman Empire were part of the Orthodox millet until the Bulgarian exarchate was established.[500] But still, the Macedonians had an especially difficult time establishing a national consciousness while others had an easier time. Andrew Rossos writes:

> Unlike other nationalisms in the Balkans or in central and eastern Europe more generally, Macedonian nationalism developed without the aid of legal, political, church, educational, or cultural institutions. Macedonian movements not only lacked any legal infrastructure, they also lacked the international sympathy, cultural aid, and, most important, benefits of open and direct diplomatic and military support accorded other Balkan nationalisms. Indeed, the nascent Macedonian nationalism, illegal at home in the theocratic Ottoman empire, and illegitimate internationally, waged a precarious struggle for survival against overwhelming odds: in appearance against the Ottoman empire, but in fact against the three expansionist Balkan states and their respective patrons among the great powers.[501]

Thus, for several reasons, the Macedonian national conscious blossomed at a different tempo and in a different manner than other ones of the Balkans.

Most Greeks refuse to accept that the people who call themselves 'Macedonian' are actually ethnic Macedonians. Consequentially, Greece refuses to accept that there are even people within their borders who consider themselves ethnic Macedonians, and instead refers to them as slavophone Greeks or bilinguals.[502] Even though they give the Macedonians a different name, they still grossly underestimate the ethnic Macedonian population statistics within their borders. Unfortunately for many Greek citizens, the Macedonian minority is not the only unrecognized minority. The only recognized minority in Greece is the Turkish Muslim minority.[503]

Misconceptions by Greeks, Bulgarians and Serbs have caused them to insist that Tito created the Macedonian identity. Greeks in particular believe that the "Macedonian identity is largely a Titoist contrivance."[504] For example, at a UN committee meeting, a Greek representative stated: "[c]oncerning the question of Macedonia, it was important to recall that it was a region divided among Greece, Bulgaria and the former State of Yugoslavia. There was no distinct Macedonian ethnicity, which was only an idea invented by Marshall Tito. There was, therefore, no Macedonian minority in

---

[499] Vladimir Andreieff Tsanoff, *Facts About Macedonians,* The New York Times, August 16, 1903: 9.
[500] Rossos, Andrew, *Macedonia and the Macedonians,* 4 (2008).
[501] *Id.* at 61.
[502] Human Rights Watch, *Denying Ethnic Identity: The Macedonians in Greece,* 1 (1994).
[503] *Id.*
[504] International Crisis Group, *Macedonia's Name: Why the Dispute Matters and How to Resolve It,* 15 (2001).

Greece[.]"[505] However, in reality, Tito simply gave Macedonians a "formal legal and institutional expression."[506] In actuality, "the ethnic origins of the Macedonian people are ancient."[507]

Not only is the Macedonian identity an ancient one, it is one that has maintained its name continuously through the centuries. Personal accounts by Michael Psellus in the 11th century demonstrate the distinct characteristics of Macedonians during the time:

> It happened that at that particular time there was a Macedonian colony living in the neighborhood of the city. Prominent among them were people who had originally lived in Adrianopolis. They were crafty individuals, saying one thing and meaning another, only too willing to take up any ridiculous project and most energetic in carrying it out, very clever at hiding their thoughts, and absolutely loyal to the agreements they made among themselves. The emperor [Constantine] treated them with complete indifference. As far as he was concerned, the lion had already been sacrificed and his claws had been drawn.[508]

> [...]

> Most of the Macedonians, being a folk who delight in arrogance and insolent bearing, more accustomed to the buffoonery of townsmen than the simplicity of the camp, most of them, I say, dismounted from their horses and started choral dances where everyone could see them. They improvised comic turns at the emperor's expense, stamping on the ground with their feet in time to their music and dancing in triumph.[509]

Still, it has only been recently that Macedonia has "asserted itself as a nation organized on a political and territorial basis."[510] Because of this previous lack of national organization, many claim that Macedonians have a lack of national identity. But "[i]ronically, the lack of national identity could also be a kind of identity and it is not by chance that the thesis of the 'floating mass' of Macedonian Slavs is often used by the Macedonian national historiography in order to assert a distinct 'ethnic character.'"[511] The fact that there were a group of people who occupied Macedonia for millennia that did not consider themselves part of the peoples that surround them indicates that they were their own ethnic group. Further, just because the Macedonian elite were slow in forming a national ethnic identity does not say anything about the peasantry, nor is it accurate to say that peasantries of other lands were "more 'awake' and nationally oriented" than the Macedonians.[512]

Still, in the 1800s, Macedonian activists "talk[ed] of a 'Macedonian movement,' which should be understood as independent national and religious emancipation[.]"[513] The

---

[505] Committee on the Elimination of Racial Discrimination.

[506] Apostolov, Mico, *The Macedonian Question -- Changes in Content Over Time*, viii (2006).

[507] Kosanic, Zoran, *Obstacle's to FYROM's Membership of NATO: A Tougher Agenda Than Expected*, 2 (2009).

[508] *Michael Psellus: Fourteen Byzantine Rulers*, 208 (1966).

[509] *Id.* at 213.

[510] Kosanic, Zoran, *Obstacle's to FYROM's Membership of NATO: A Tougher Agenda Than Expected*, 2 (2009).

[511] Marinov, Tchavdar, *We, the Macedonians: The Paths of Macedonian Supra-Nationalism (1878-1912)*, in *We, the People: Politics of National Peculiarity in Southeastern Europe* by Diana Mishkova, 109 (2009).

[512] *Id.* at 110.

[513] Rossos, Andrew, *Macedonia and the Macedonians*, 86 (2008).

local people in Macedonia began developing "a distinct Macedonian loyalty."[514] Further, the discovery of "a poem on Macedonia, a proclamation for the Macedonian people, and a memorandum to …free Macedonia from its 'misfortunes'" by the Russian historian Zhila Lenina in 1829 in St. Petersburg, demonstrates that the Macedonian concept is not new or any less modern than that of its neighboring countries.[515] Rather, the Macedonian identity was suppressed because it was "a critical element in consolidating territorial control (for Serbs and Greeks) and challenging it (for revanchist Bulgarians)."[516] Still, the evidence indicates that Macedonians were a separate and distinct ethnic group.

Many people have defined and described the Macedonians in their own ways. Here is a description by HN Brailsford:

> "The Reality behind the whole muddle of racial conflicts, beyond the Chauvinism of the Balkan peoples and the calculations of the greater Powers, is the unrewarded figure of the Macedonian peasant, harried, exploited, enslaved, careless of national programmes, and anxious only for a day when he may keep his warm sheepskin coat upon his back, give his daughter in marriage without dishonour, and eat in peace the bread of his own unceasing labour."[517]

Or, as Rebecca West said in her journey through Yugoslavia:

> "…I had recognized in Macedonia a uniquely beautiful life of the people. When the Macedonians loved or sang or worshipped God or watched their sheep, they brought to the business in hand poetic minds that would not believe in appearances and probed them for reality, that possessed as a birthright that quality which Keats believed to be above all others in forming a 'Man of Achievement, especially in Literature, and which Shakespeare possessed so enormously.' 'Negative Capability' he called it, and it made a man 'capable of being in uncertainties, doubts, without any irritale reaching after fact and reason.'"[518]

From the American legal world in 1911, a Yale Law Review Article listed Macedonians, among Armenians, Finns, and Poles, as oppressed peoples.[519] Note that the terms "Finn" and "Pole" are terms used to describe ethnicity, not simply geographical or national adjectives. Even American courts labeled Macedonians as their own ethnic people. A 1917 New York case found that "both parties are Macedonian."[520] A Supreme Court of Minnesota decision from 1912 stated that "the plaintiff was a Macedonian."[521] An Ohio court in 1908 stated that "George was a Macedonian."[522]

Sometimes scholars tended to label Macedonia as a heterogeneous country. But the reality is that the "famous mixed character of Macedonia…did not differ much from other regions in Eastern and Southeastern Europe like the Banat and Vojvodina, Transylvania,

---

[514] Marinov, Tchavdar, *We, the Macedonians: The Paths of Macedonian Supra-Nationalism (1878-1912)*, in *We, the People: Politics of National Peculiarity in Southeastern Europe* by Diana Mishkova, 111 (2009).

[515] Wieland, Carsten, *One Macedonia with Three Faces: Domestic Debates and Nation Concept*, 7.

[516] International Crisis Group, *Macedonia's Name: Why the Dispute Matters and How to Resolve It*, 11-12 (2001).

[517] Glenny, Misha, *The Balkans: Nationalism, War and The Great Power, 1804 – 1999*, 205 (2000).

[518] West, Rebecca, Black Lamb and Grey Falcon: A Journey Through Yugoslavia, 482 (1941).

[519] Tryon, James L., The Hague Conferences, April 1911, Yale Law Journal, 20 YLJ 470, 477.

[520] In re Ylia, 233 F. 476, 477. 1916.

[521] Vaneff v. Great Northern Ry. Co., 120 Minn. 18, 19. 1912.

[522] Louis C. Mengert, In re., 1908 WL 700, Pg. 4. 1908.

Dobroudja..."[523] and Greece. The reason Macedonia is generally thought of as the heterogeneous nation of the Balkans probably had to do with the politics and events of the 19th and 20th century regarding the competing interests of Balkan nations to exert influence and dominance in Macedonia. During this time, Bulgaria, Serbia and Greece attempted to eradicate a sense of being Macedonian through education, changing surnames, and negating the use of the Macedonian language.[524] Before the dawn of the 20th century, Greece had established over 1400 schools in Macedonia,[525] teaching kids that they were Greeks. The amount of money the Greeks spent on education in geographic Macedonia was proportionally greater than what they spent on Greece at the time.[526] Further, Serbia had 100 schools promoting Serbian nationalism in geographic Macedonia while Bulgaria established 700 doing the same,[527] of which 200 were in Aegean Macedonia.[528] With 2200 schools in Macedonia teaching children they were one nationality rather than another, it was not difficult to believe that Macedonia was a heterogeneous country.

But this was the reality – the Serbs, Bulgarians and Greeks struggled to convert the Macedonians:

> In the second half of the nineteenth century, the three competing states ... claimed the Macedonians on ethnic grounds, purposely confusing church affiliation with ethno-linguistic belonging. All three had recognized ''national'' Orthodox churches and hence millets in the theocratic Ottoman state. These national churches could operate freely in Ottoman Macedonia: establish parishes and schools and, especially after 1870, serve as instruments of their respective nationalist drives and propaganda there. The Macedonians did not and could not set up their own church and therefore could not organize and conduct legally any religious and educational activities under their national name...''The Serbians pointed to certain characteristics of their grammar and to their 'slava' festival as proof of their Serbian origin. The Bulgarians argued that physiologically the Macedonians were closer to them than to the Serbs and that the Macedonian language was in reality a Bulgarian dialect. And the Greeks claimed that many Macedonians considered themselves to be Greeks and therefore they referred to them as Slavophone Greeks.''[529]

In the late 1920s, Greece took this assimilation and propaganda campaign to new heights. After publishing a booklet in 1920 titled 'Advice on the Change of Names of Municipalities and Villages,'[530] the Greeks spent the decade changing the history of Aegean Macedonia. All Macedonian place names were changed to Greek ones; all ethnic Macedonian schools were closed; and Macedonian church texts were painted over with Greek texts.[531]

Life became harder for Macedonians in Greece after World War II. The

---

[523] Marinov, Tchavdar, *We, the Macedonians: The Paths of Macedonian Supra-Nationalism (1878-1912)*, in *We, the People: Politics of National Peculiarity in Southeastern Europe* by Diana Mishkova, 110-111 (2009).

[524] International Crisis Group, *Macedonia's Name: Breaking the Deadlock*, 2 (2009).

[525] Poulton, Hugh, *The Balkans: Minorities and States in Conflict*, 47 (1994).

[526] *Id.*

[527] *Id.*

[528] *Id.* at 176.

[529] Rossos, Andrew, *Macedonia and the Macedonians*, 73-74 (2008).

[530] Medichkov, Peter, *Greek Acts Against the Macedonians: 1912-1994*, http://maknews.com/html/articles/medichkov/medichkov_report.htm .

[531] Underdown, Michael, *Background to the Macedonian Question*, 4 (1994).

Macedonian region was re-colonized with Greeks; Macedonians could only use Greek names; and Macedonians had to confirm in public that they did not speak Macedonian.[532] Actually, in 1938, a legal act banned the Macedonian language in Greece.[533] One Yugoslav official in the 1940s stated that "the chauvinistic tendencies of the Hellenic government are dangerous to the peace of the world" when speaking about the terror being forced upon Macedonians in Aegean Macedonia.[534] As a matter of fact, a Macedonian "in Greece ... speak[ing] of united Macedonia [was] enough to convince a Greek that he [was] a dangerous and undesirable citizen."[535] In 1954, Macedonians were removed from all official positions in the Greek government.[536] These policies caused Macedonians to flee to the USA, Canada, and Australia.[537] Also, in 1982 and 1985, two Greek Acts prohibited Macedonians from a right to return to Greece and a right to regain their property.[538] Both of those acts violated provisions in the Universal Declaration of Human Rights.[539] Further, Greece does not respect the conditions on treatment of minorities that is required of would-be members of EU and NATO.[540] For example, in 1990, a Greek court denied Macedonians from establishing a cultural association because some of its founding members stated that a Macedonian ethnic identity existed in Greece, and because another founding member would not state in court that he was an ethnic Greek.[541] The court claimed that a society affirming the existence of Macedonians in Greece is against Greece's national interests.[542]

There are a few significant international documents that Greece has signed onto to which they do not adhere. First, there is the 1990 Document of the Copenhagen Meeting of the Conference on the Human Dimension of the Conference on Security and Cooperation in Europe (CSCE), which states:

> To belong to a national minority is a matter of a person's individual choice and no disadvantage may arise from the exercise of such choice. Persons belonging to national minorities have the right freely to express, preserve and develop their ethnic, cultural, linguistic or religious identity and to maintain and develop their culture in all its aspects, free of any attempts at assimilation against their will.[543]

Then there is the UN Declaration on the Rights of Persons Belonging to National or Ethnic, Religious and Linguistic Minorities, which was adopted in 1992, and of which in part states:

---

[532] *Id.* at 5.
[533] *The Human Rights Situation of Macedonians in Greece and Australia,*
http://www.pollitecon.com/html/life/The_Human_Rights_Situation_of_Macedonians_in_Greece_and_Australia.html . Jul. 1993.
[534] *Tension Increases Over Macedonia.* The Leader Post. Sep. 7, 1946: 1.
[535] King, William B., *Trouble is Brewing in the Balkans.* The Milwaukee Journal. Jul. 29th, 1945: 46.
[536] Underdown, Michael, *Background to the Macedonian Question,* 5 (1994).
[537] *Id.*
[538] *Id.*
[539] *Id.*
[540] International Crisis Group, *Macedonia's Name: Breaking the Deadlock,* 7 (2009).
[541] Human Rights Watch, *Denying Ethnic Identity: The Macedonians in Greece,* 20 (1994).
[542] *Id.* at 21.
[543] *Id.* at 18.

States shall protect the existence and the national or ethnic, cultural, religious and linguistic identity of minorities within their respective territories and shall encourage conditions for the promotion of that identity.[544]

....

Persons belonging to . . . minorities have the right to enjoy their own culture . . . in private and in public, freely and without interference or any form of discrimination.[545]

....

Persons belonging to minorities have the right to establish and maintain their own associations.[546]

There is also the Vienna Declaration of 1993, of which Appendix II states:

States should create the conditions necessary for persons belonging to national minorities to develop their culture, while preserving their religion, traditions and customs. These persons must be able to use their language both in private and in public and should be able to use it, under certain conditions, in their relations with the public authorities.[547]

The official Greek position is that Greece is an ethnically homogenous country,[548] so it is not surprising that Greece denies the existence of other ethnic minorities within its borders. For example, in 2008, the European Court of Human Rights ruled that Greece could not prevent "two groups in a Muslim-populated region of northern Greece to [from] defin[ing] themselves as 'Turkish.'"[549]

Furthermore, in the early 1990s, the Greek Prime Minister Mitsotakis affirmed that Greece's Macedonia policy had more to do with the fear of creating a minority problem in Greece, and not really that much to do with the name of Macedonia.[550] Greece states that there can be no Macedonians in northern Greece because, aside from the fact that they believe there are no such people called ethnic Macedonians, the people who call themselves ethnic Macedonian were all gone by 1949.[551] This belief caused a mayor of Florina (Aegean Macedonia) to state: "There are no Macedonians in Greece; everyone is Greek."[552] Yet, the government of Macedonia insists that there are no less than 230,000 ethnic Macedonians in Greece, which is about 10% of the Aegean Macedonian population; and the US State Department confirms that there are at least 50,000 people who speak the Macedonian tongue.[553] Of course, the US estimate does not suggest that this is the number of ethnic Macedonians, as it does not take into account the fact that ethnic Macedonians were not allowed to speak Macedonian for many decades, which meant that Macedonian children could not learn Macedonian.

Still, other research shows differently. An independent study by a German linguist

---

[544] *Id.* at 19.

[545] *Id.* at 21.

[546] *Id.*

[547] *Id.* at 19.

[548] *Id.* at. 11.

[549] *Athens to Appeal EU Thrace Ruling.*
http://archive.ekathimerini.com/4dcgi/_w_articles_politics_100008_19/06/2008_97801 . June, 19th, 2008.

[550] Axt, Heinz-Jurgen et. al., *The Greek Macedonian Name Dispute -- Reconciliation through Europeanization?,* 11 (2006).

[551] Human Rights Watch, *Denying Ethnic Identity: The Macedonians in Greece,* 11 (1994).

[552] Human Rights Watch, *Denying Ethnic Identity: The Macedonians in Greece,* 12 (1994).

[553] *Id.* at 13. Note: the US State Department called it a "Slavic tongue."

determined that, as of 2003, there were around 200,000 speakers of Macedonian-Slav dialects in Aegean Macedonia.[554] Greece denies this and states the maximum number of such speakers was 41,000 in 1951 and believes that this number has drastically declined since then.[555] But one Western report in 1992 suggested that many cities in Aegean Macedonia "do not have any indigenous Greek inhabitants at all."[556]

It is true that today's modern Macedonian is a Slavic-based language.[557] But Greece has denied this and simply says that the people in Aegean Macedonia are Slav speaking ethnic Greeks.[558] What this means, is still not clear. Are these people ethnically Greek who have managed to hold onto the exact language of the invading Slavic tribes of the 6th century, but which is a language clearly distinct from any current Slavic based language, such as Macedonian, Bulgarian, Serbian, Russian, or Polish? It is anyone's guess. But Greece suggests these people who speak Macedonian are really agents of Skopje, and they know this by the way these ethnic Macedonians behave and what they say.[559] Currently, Greece is pressuring Macedonians not to "display their identity or speak Macedonian."[560] This contradicts Greece's views of the 1920s, when Greece was the first Balkan nation to publish a Macedonian language primer for its Macedonian minority in Aegean Macedonia,[561] even though the Serbs and Bulgarians protested this policy to the League of Nations.[562] Perhaps the fact that people suggested publishing such primer in Greece was because the number of Macedonian speakers in geographic Macedonia as of 1912 was estimated to be about 1.15 million, according to the British Foreign Office, which was four times the number of Greek speakers[563] and the largest ethno-linguistic group in this region.[564] When Greece annexed Aegean Macedonia, it came with no less than 330,000 Macedonians,[565] and an additional 40,000 ethnic Macedonian who possessed the Muslim faith.[566] Even through mass expulsions and exoduses of Macedonians through the 1920s, the Governorship-General of Thessaloniki and of Thrace estimated there were over 180,000 Slav-Macedonians in Aegean Macedonia.[567] Some estimates in an Austrian atlas put the number of Macedonians in Greece at 500,000.[568]

---

[554] Axt, Heinz-Jurgen et. al., *The Greek Macedonian Name Dispute -- Reconciliation through Europeanization?*, 11 (2006).
[555] Human Rights Watch, *Denying Ethnic Identity: The Macedonians in Greece*, 13 (1994).
[556] *The Human Rights Situation of Macedonians in Greece and Australia*, http://www.pollitecon.com/html/life/The_Human_Rights_Situation_of_Macedonians_in_Greece_and_Australia.html . Jul. 1993.
[557] Underdown, Michael, *Background to the Macedonian Question*, 6 (1994).
[558] *Id.*
[559] Human Rights Watch, *Denying Ethnic Identity: The Macedonians in Greece*, 50 (1994).
[560] Gay McDougall Mission to Greece, *Promotion and Protection of All Human Rights, Civil, Political, Economic, Social and Cultural Rights, Including the Right to Development*, 14 (2009).
[561] Vangelov, Ognen, *The Greek Veto the Macedonian Identity*, 6.
[562] Medichkov, Peter, *Greek Acts Against the Macedonians: 1912-1994*, http://maknews.com/html/articles/medichkov/medichkov_report.htm .
[563] Rossos, Andrew, *Macedonia and the Macedonians*, 5 (2008).
[564] *Id.* at 18.
[565] *Id.* at 5.
[566] Poulton, Hugh, *The Balkans: Minorities and States in Conflict*, 175 (1994).
[567] Kontogiorgi, Elisabeth, *Population Exchange in Greek Macedonia : The Forced Settlement of Refugees, 1922-1930*, 235 (2006).
[568] *Greek Census in 1921 Shows 500,000 Macedonians*. http://macedoniaonline.eu/content/view/2236/45/ . Jul. 9th, 2008.

Regardless, ethnic Macedonians in Greece believe that they are of the same ethnic descent as Macedonians in Macedonia and have a different culture than ethnic Greeks.[569] As Aegean Macedonians insist, their language dates back to 9th century Old Church Slavonic,[570] and Bulgarian and Greek linguists are the only ones that do not recognize this language.[571] One ethnic Macedonian in Aegean Macedonia reported that Macedonians do not have permission to teach Macedonian as a class because the Greek government states the language does not exist.[572] This continues to occur even though the United Nations Declaration on the Rights of Persons Belonging to National or Ethnic, Religious and Linguistic Minorities says that countries "should take appropriate measures so that, wherever possible, persons belonging to minorities may have adequate opportunities to learn their mother tongue or to have instruction in their mother tongue."[573] According to the words of Ilce Musarevski, a Macedonian human rights activist in Australia, "[c]oloured people in South Africa have more human rights than Macedonians in Greece, the so-called cradle of democracy[.]"[574]

Greece has not ratified the Framework Agreement for the Protection of Ethnic Minorities or the European Declaration on Minority Languages and Religions.[575] Perhaps this allows Greece to conjure that the Macedonian language is really an idiom of Turkish, Albanian, Bulgarian and Greek.[576] Still, the Greeks' intolerance of the use of the Macedonian language is evidenced by one Greek schoolteacher's testimonial:

> During breaks in high school, kids speak Macedonian to each other. They speak Macedonian with me, too, because they know I'm Macedonian. Whether a kid gets in trouble for speaking Macedonian depends on the teacher--if the teacher decides to report it, the kid's parents may be called in. Other teachers are open-minded, and don't report such things. In the old days, when I was a child (I'm thirty-eight now), teachers would hit kids with sticks if they spoke Macedonian, and would say things like, "You dirty Bulgarians, you'll never learn Greek."[577]

Further, in the late 1980s, very young children only in Aegean Macedonia were required to attend "'integrated kindergartens' to prevent them from learning the Macedonian language and culture."[578]

Greece eventually issued a short period of time for ethnic Macedonians to come visit Aegean Macedonia in 2003; but the mood was very tense, as highlighted in one ethnic Macedonian's experience with a border official:

---

[569] Human Rights Watch, *Denying Ethnic Identity: The Macedonians in Greece*, 1 (1994).
[570] *Id.* at 36.
[571] *Id.*
[572] *Id.* at 41.
[573] *Id.* at 44.
[574] Warne, Leslie, *We Exist, Say Illawarra Macedonians*, http://www.greenleft.org.au/node/2031 Mar. 11th, 1992.
[575] Kondonis, Haralambos, *Bilateral Relations Between Greece and the Former Yugoslav Republic of Macedonia*, 80.
[576] Human Rights Watch, *Denying Ethnic Identity: The Macedonians in Greece*, 37 (1994).
[577] *Id.* at 41.
[578] *The Human Rights Situation of Macedonians in Greece and Australia*, http://www.pollitecon.com/html/life/The_Human_Rights_Situation_of_Macedonians_in_Greece_and_Australia.html . Jul. 1993.

"What's your name?" the border guard barked.

"My name is Georgi," said Mr Donevski, who runs the Skopje-based world organisation of refugee children from Greece.

"No, your Greek name!"

"I think it's Giorgos Antoniou, but I have not used it since I left your country in 1948."

"And your birthplace?"

"Baptchor," he beamed, using the Slav name for his ancestral home.

"There is no Baptchor" the guard said. "There never was a Baptchor. There is only the Greek village Pimenikon. I will give you a visa to visit Pimenikon."[579]

Of the over 600 exiled ethnic Macedonians who took advantage of the temporary lifting of the ban on them, the Greek Deputy Foreign Minister, Andreas Loverdos, said that "[t]hey are the civil war's innocent victims[;] [...] [t]his is a humanitarian measure, a first step toward righting the wrongs of the past."[580] Yet, 150 other Macedonians were denied entrance into Greece because they would not change the Macedonian birthplaces listed on their passports to their recently changed Greek names.[581]

Despite this, as late as 2009, the Report of the Council of Europe stated that Greece was not providing basic rights and freedoms to minorities.[582] Even though "[c]ommunity representatives note that traditional names continue to be in common usage and call for reinstatement and the official usage of a dual nomenclature...,"[583] language rights are denied to Macedonians. Much of these troubling trends are noted in Greece Representative Telalian's remarks and summary of her remarks in recent UN Committee meetings:

> In certain villages in the northern Greek region of Macedonia, there was a very small number of persons who claimed to have a distinct ethnic and national "Macedonian" identity, and who wished to be recognized as a minority in Greece. Those claims had been rejected by all Greek Governments as being politically motivated and having nothing to do with human rights; they also created a climate of insecurity and tension. Moreover, there were Greeks in that same area who spoke a Slavic oral idiom, but had never considered themselves as having a distinct ethnic or national identity.[...] The use of the name "Macedonian" to identify the existence of a national minority in Greece could not be accepted for the same reasons that Greece could not accept the use of the name Macedonia by a neighbouring country.[584]
>
> [...]
>
> The use of the term "Macedonian", which had great meaning for the people of Greece, was misleading when used by a small group wishing to associate itself with the Macedonian nation and to claim national minority rights in Greece. As to the participation of the so-called Macedonian minority, through its Rainbow Association, in Greek political life, she [Ms. Telalian] said that it had increased by a very small percentage in recent years

---

[579] Smith, Helena, *Bittersweet Return for Greek Civil War's Lost Victims: Greece is Allowing Ethnic Macedonians Exiled in the 1940s to Revisit Their Homes for the First Time*, http://www.guardian.co.uk/world/2003/oct/17/greece . Oct. 17, 2003.

[580] *Id.*

[581] *Id.*

[582] Vangeli, Anastas, *Antiquity Musing: Reflections on the Greco-Macedonian Symbolic Contest over the Narratives of the Ancient Past*, 16 (2009).

[583] Gay McDougall Mission to Greece, *Promotion and Protection of All Human Rights, Civil, Political, Economic, Social and Cultural Rights, Including the Right to Development*, 13 (2009).

[584] International Covenant on Civil and Political Rights. *Summary Record of the 2268th Meeting*, March, 2005: 6.

following the parliamentary elections.[585]

[...]

With regard to claims made by other minorities, she [Ms. Telalian] said that subjective claims made by a small number of persons who belong to a distinct ethnic or cultural group, unless linked to relevant objective criteria, were not sufficient to impose an obligation on a State to recognize that group officially as a minority and afford it relevant protection. Ethnic, cultural, linguistic or religious differences alone did not necessarily make a group a national or ethnic minority. Consequently, claims that the Greek Government failed to recognize "Macedonians" as a national or linguistic minority were unsubstantiated and threatened to create tension over existing identities in the region. It also caused confusion over the name "Macedonian", which was used by hundreds of thousands of Greek Macedonians living in northern Greece. Any attempt to declare "Macedonians" a small group in the region threatened to distort the cultural heritage of the 2.5 million Greek Macedonians. In that context, the non-recognition of such a group as a national minority did not imply discriminatory treatment or the creation of a protection gap.[586]

[...]

There was no Macedonian minority officially recognized as such in Greece, and it was unfortunate that certain activists were seeking to convince the international community otherwise. The truth was that a group of persons in the north of Greece spoke a Slavonic dialect, but they had never said that they did not consider themselves Greek nor had they claimed a different ethnic identify. In conformity with the principle of self-identification, the desire of those persons, who had not requested affiliation with any country other than Greece, should be respected. For that reason Greece did not recognize the existence of a Macedonian minority in its territory.[587]

To this day, Greece continues to disobey the ruling of the 1998 European Court of Human Rights, which "found Greece in violation of Article 11 of the European Convention on Human Rights relating to freedom of association."[588] Greece claims that the issue is still pending before its Supreme Court,[589] which would mean the right of an ethnic Macedonian group in Greece to form a cultural association is taking over two decades to litigate.

Anthropologists have concluded that a Macedonian minority has existed in northern Greece since at least the 1800s.[590] Further, the Human Rights Watch acknowledges that there are two types of citizens in Aegean Macedonia: Macedonians of Slavic descent, who have been there since the 6th century AD; and ethnic Greeks, who resettled there in the 1920s.[591] Apparently, so do some Greeks (political opposition groups

---

[585] International Covenant on Civil and Political Rights. *Summary Record of the 2269th Meeting.* March, 2005: 6.
[586] International Convention on the Elimination of all Forms of Racial Discrimination. *Summary Record of the 1944th Meeting.* August 2009: 4.
[587] International Convention on the Elimination of all Forms of Racial Discrimination. *Summary Record of the First Part of the 1456th Meeting.* March 2001: 8.
[588] Gay McDougall Mission to Greece, *Promotion and Protection of All Human Rights, Civil, Political, Economic, Social and Cultural Rights, Including the Right to Development*, 13 (2009).
[589] *Id.*
[590] Human Rights Watch, *Denying Ethnic Identity: The Macedonians in Greece*, 1 (1994).
[591] *Id.* at 5.

to the main Greek parties). Still, only the Macedonians with Slavic ancestry fear the repercussions of demonstrating their identity.[592]

Macedonia as its own nation, free or not

Not only is it imperative to show that the Macedonians were and are their own ethnic people, it is vital to demonstrate that the Macedonian nation has existed continuously through centuries of occupation. A Greek Foreign Ministry letter to the former UN Secretary General Butros Butros-Ghali stated that the Macedonians breaking away from Yugoslavia had the "aim of creating a new, historically non-existing country, with territorial pretensions as its fundamental policy[…]"[593] The evidence shows, however, that the 'Macedonian nation' was not a Tito idea or creation. As two British students in 1921 put it: "…in observing the modern Macedonia, one is studying the type amongst whom St. Paul preached and traveled."[594]

Macedonia appeared for the first time in the US census in 1860, when Richard Casaus listed Macedonia as his place of birth.[595] Then in Tsanoff's 1903 letter we also confront evidence of the desire of a free Macedonia. He wrote: "The only Macedonia that an American can champion is a free Macedonia."[596] Another 1903 article in the *New York Times* suggests that Macedonia was once a free territory in the late 1880s, which further shows that it was not a Tito creation. "The Macedonians have apparently not forgotten the taste which twenty-five years ago they had of liberty, when for four short months they were an independent people. It will be remembered that …Russia secured for Macedonia liberty from Turkish misrule, and gave them the luxury of national independence."[597]

But probably the most damning *New York Times* article to the notion that Tito was the one who first sponsored a Macedonian nation is Harvard scholar V.K. Sugareff's 1919 letter logically and emotionally pleading for an independent Macedonian state:

> "Those of us Macedonians, whose families have been scattered to the four winds as a result of the political unrest in that country, are quite convinced the Macedonian question has not been presented to the American public in the light of an untainted justice. Should Macedonia be subjected to another prewar regime, it will be a bitter disappointment to hundreds of us who denned the khaki to defend the honor of the United States and her broad principles which the Allies ultimately adopted. [A solution that is] "most acceptable to the Macedonians, is that Macedonia should be established as an independent state."[598]

Along with stating that self-determination would not work in Macedonia because it would take many years to rid the country of outside interference,[599] Sugareff added: "Had the organic law of 1866 been applied to Macedonia, as provided by Article 23 of the Berlin

---

[592] Gay McDougall Mission to Greece, *Promotion and Protection of All Human Rights, Civil, Political, Economic, Social and Cultural Rights, Including the Right to Development*, 14 (2009).

[593] Apostolov, Mico, *The Macedonian Question -- Changes in Content Over Time*, x-xi (2006).

[594] Mazower, Mark, *The Balkans: A Short History*, 14 (2002).

[595] Sinadinoski, Dusan, *Early Macedonian Immigration to the United States*. http://www.utrinski.com.mk/?ItemID=95480AD35DDC4744A487339E580A9F56

[596] Vladimir Andreieff Tsanoff, *Facts About Macedonians*. The New York Times. August 16, 1903: 9.

[597] "Macedonia's Brief Freedom." The New York Times. March 15, 1903. Pg. 6.

[598] VK Sugareff *"A Free Macedonia: A Government Like Switzerland's Being Urged Upon the Paris Conference."* New York Times. April 27, 1919: 38.

[599] *Id.*

Treaty, Macedonia would have been an embryonic autonomous state."[600] He even suggested that a solution would be to give Macedonia autonomy similar to that of the Switzerland government.[601]

Further, it is also the differences of Macedonia and the Macedonians from her neighbors that promote the notion that it is and always has been a separate and distinct nation. Throughout the beginning of the 19th century, Macedonia remained stabilized by Turkish misgovernance in the same medieval conditions which existed there since the 1300s.[602] "Macedonia perhaps should be looked on as a museum not typical of the life outside it."[603] Its isolation and separation from surrounding nations only lends more support to Macedonia being its own nation.

American court cases also shed light as to the nationhood status of Macedonia. Even though Macedonia was thrown from one occupier's control to another, the court cases clearly show that American judges felt and thought Macedonia was its own nation and country. One court decision in 1906 stemming from the Supreme Court of Kansas, referred to Macedonia as the 'Province of Macedonia' when discussing the facts of a previous case in 1903.[604] Of particular importance is how the judge capitalized *Province*, given the term Macedonia more than simply a geographical connotation. A Supreme Court of Illinois decision in 1917 also shows that Macedonia was its own nation and country in two ways. First, the decision states that the plaintiff, Simonoff, was a native of Macedonia.[605] Second, and incredibly insightful, the judge goes on to say that when Simonoff was in Macedonia, Macedonia and Serbia were at war with Austria-Hungary.[606] A prior decision in 1916 regarding the Simonoff case stated that Simonoff was leaving "for his home country of Macedonia."[607] This shows that Macedonia was not a part of Serbia, or rather, any other nation. It shows that Macedonia was its own country, fighting alongside Serbia, in a war against the Austro-Hungarian Empire. The US Ninth Circuit Court of Appeals also issued a case in 1928 that demonstrates this independent Macedonian nation. The judge wrote the following:

> The evidence taken in said proceedings conclusively shows that the petitioner is a native of Macedonia, which was a Turkish province at the time of his birth, and it is a matter of historical knowledge, of which the court should take judicial notice, that, since the year 1919, Macedonia has been partitioned and divided up among several countries. It is then averred on information and belief that the government of the republic of Greece has refused to issue any passport for the removal of the petitioner to Greece, and will refuse to allow him to enter that country, for the reason that is not a native or citizen thereof ...[even though]...he was born in Veria, Macedonia, formerly a part of the Turkish Empire, and now a part of the Greek Republic.[608]

Several other court cases indicate that throughout the early 20th century, even with Macedonia under Ottoman rule and then subsequently divided into several parts, plaintiffs

---

[600] *Id.*

[601] *Id.*

[602] West, Rebecca, *Black Lamb and Grey Falcon: A Journey Through Yugoslavia.* 482 (1941).

[603] *Id.*

[604] Atchison, T. & S. F. RY. CO. v. Fajardo et al., 86 P. 301, 303 also (74 Kan. 314). July 6, 1906.

[605] Simonoff v. Granite City Nat. Bank, 279 Ill. 248, 249. 1917.

[606] Simonoff v. Granite City Nat. Bank, 279 Ill. 248, 250. 1917.

[607] Sotir Simonoff for use of Illio Simonoff v. Granite City National Bank, 1916 WL 2728, Pg. 1. 1916.

[608] Caranica v. Nagle, 28 F.2d 955, 956. 1928.

and defendants in American courts still referred to Macedonia as a country. In a 1932 Supreme Court of Michigan case, the record shows that the defendant's "ultimate European destination was Macedonia."[609] And in a United States tax court, the petitioner stated that he visited the countries of Greece and Macedonia in 1914.[610] Clearly this helps to demonstrate that Macedonia was still referred to as a country by people outside of the Balkans, especially as a country separate than Greece.

What all this evidence shows is that Tito did not create a Macedonian nation or state out of thin air. Tito's actions did help Macedonia achieve independence, something it had been struggling to do for centuries. Whatever Tito's motives were for doing such are beside the point and beyond the scope of this article. What we do know is that "Macedonia was one of the first areas to be conquered by the Ottoman Empires and one of the last to be freed;"[611] yet, it was still an area considered separate and distinct from surrounding areas.

Greece and the Greeks

Necessary to resolving the Macedonian identity question is not only asking who the Macedonians are, but asking 'who are the Greeks?' The idea of the modern Greek state stems from the Treaty of Westphalia in 1648, and this had little to do with ethnicity.[612] But the actual construction of the Greek state comes much later. One author describes how the construction of the Greek state began to form, and how it had practically nothing to do with ethnic affiliation:

> In the Greek case, the desire to construct a state came initially from the Greek commercial diaspora scattered around the Mediterranean and Black Seas and in the cities of Central and Western Europe allied to the romantic aspiration, shared with "philhellenic" Western intellectuals (most famously England's Lord Byron), to liberate Balkan Christians from the Ottoman Turks and, hopefully, to reestablish the glory of ancient Greece. If there was a concentration of identifiably Greek people living in the southern part of the Balkan Peninsula, many if not most Greeks (of either linguistic or religious qualification) lived scattered well beyond this territory. Of course, quite what constituted a "Greek" as opposed to a Balkan Christian or even a Turkish Christian remained very much in doubt. As Greece was made, so were the Greeks.[613]

Further, the Great Powers of the 1800s had much influence in creating an independent Greek state in 1830.[614] This "Greek state was a largely foreign enterprise financed by Britain and France[,] and in the hands of a Bavarian prince and administrators."[615] Actually, it was not until 1843, after a coup d'état, that a Greek state "arm[ed] with a powerful mythic origin" emerged.[616] Many of these myths included a Greek state that

---

[609] Central State Bank v. Zelli, 244 N.W. 503, 503. 1932.

[610] Zareh Nubar v. Commissioner of Internal Revenu, 13 T.C. 566, 568. 1949.

[611] Poulton, Hugh, *The Balkans: Minorities and States in Conflict*, 277 (1994).

[612] Underdown, Michael, *Background to the Macedonian Question*, 12 (1994).

[613] Agnew, John, *No Borders, No Nations: Making Greece in Macedonia*, 97 Annals of the Association of American Geographers 2, 2007: 404.

[614] Vangeli, Anastas, *Antiquity Musing: Reflections on the Greco-Macedonian Symbolic Contest over the Narratives of the Ancient Past*, 15 (2009).

[615] Agnew, John, *No Borders, No Nations: Making Greece in Macedonia*, 97 Annals of the Association of American Geographers 2, 2007: 404.

[616] *Id.*

encompassed practically the entire Balkan region and southern Italy, including Sicily.[617] In reality, the Greek nation of the mid-1800s only consisted of present-day southern Greece,[618] and not Aegean Macedonia.

Modern day Greeks, additionally, are not descended from ancient Greeks.[619] The ancient Greeks probably left Greece by the end of the 4th century AD, with newcomers occupying Greece.[620]It was not until about 500 years later when the descendants of these Greeks returned to Greece and assimilated the Slavs and Albanians (who had previously settled there) into Greeks.[621] An Austrian historian of the 1800s produced much literature explaining how modern Greeks are not related to the ancient Greeks,[622] especially concerning racial affinity, and "viewed them ... as a mix of Slavs and Albanians."[623] Another historian demonstrated that the ancient Greek civilization, which had Eastern and African roots, was practically wiped out.[624] Modern Greeks just happened to appropriate ancient Greek cultural symbols because they lived on lands of the ancient Greeks.[625] Further, most 19th century Greeks did not consider themselves Hellenes, and rather spoke variations of Slavic, the Vlach, and the Albanian languages.[626]

Greece was extremely ethnically and culturally diverse in the 1800s.[627] "[W]hen the Greek State was formed in 1829[,] it consisted of exactly the same ethnic identities that the Republic of Macedonia had in 1991."[628] Athens, the modern day Greek capitol, was 24 percent ethnic Albanian and 32 percent ethnic Turk during the 1800s;[629] which means that over half the Athenian population was not ethnically Greek. When a Greek war of liberation occurred in the 1820s, several of the heroes were Albanians, not ethnic Greeks.[630] The ethnic Greeks who did participate in the war, however, believed "they were closer to Rome than to Greece ... they saw themselves as the heirs of the Byzantium. [...] [t]hey fought as Christians against the unbelieving Muslims, as Romans against" the Turks.[631] Further, the inhabitants of Thessaloniki at the turn of the 20th century were 60% Jewish and less than 20% Greek.[632] Finally, most of the Greeks in Aegean Macedonia were resettled there throughout the 20th century from Turkey and other parts of Greece, so

---

[617] *Id.*

[618] *Id.*

[619] Underdown, Michael, *Background to the Macedonian Question*, 12 (1994).

[620] Schteppan, Hans L., *Comedy: Greek By Name*. http://maknews.com/html/articles/stefov/stefov121.html . February, 2008.

[621] *Id.*

[622] Vangeli, Anastas, *Antiquity Musing: Reflections on the Greco-Macedonian Symbolic Contest over the Narratives of the Ancient Past*, 29 (2009).

[623] Agnew, John, *No Borders, No Nations: Making Greece in Macedonia*, 97 Annals of the Association of American Geographers 2, 2007: 407.

[624] Vangeli, Anastas, *Antiquity Musing: Reflections on the Greco-Macedonian Symbolic Contest over the Narratives of the Ancient Past*, 29 (2009).

[625] Underdown, Michael, *Background to the Macedonian Question*, 12 (1994).

[626] *Id.*

[627] Vangeli, Anastas, *Antiquity Musing: Reflections on the Greco-Macedonian Symbolic Contest over the Narratives of the Ancient Past*, 29 (2009).

[628] Stefov, Risto, *Greek-Macedonian Name Dispute*. http://maknews.com/html/articles/stefov/Greek-MacedonianNameDisputeSimplefied.html . (2007).

[629] Karlsson, Ingmar, *What is a Nation?* Global Political Trends Center, 4.

[630] *Id.*

[631] *Id.*

[632] *Id.* at 5.

how those Greeks could be the inheritors of ancient Macedonian culture, history, and ancestry remains mysterious.[633]

But the Greek national myth stresses continuity between the ancient Hellenic world and today's Greece.[634] With the idea that Alexander the Great was truly a Greek, the 19th century Greeks had a justification for including the Macedonian territory in the national Greek agenda.[635] Capturing Macedonia also brought "together the ancient and Byzantine conceptions of the Greek nation, thus reconciling the Church and the modern nation."[636] Spread was the fear that Greece would be mutilated without its lungs -- Macedonia.[637] Thus, it is no surprise today that when a scholar in the 1990s wanted to publicize this ethnic and cultural diversity of Greece and Aegean Macedonia, specifically about the Slavic speaking people of Greece who consider themselves Macedonian and not Greek,[638] she "received death threats and Cambridge University Press refused to publish her book because Greek nationalists promised violent retribution."[639] Greek human rights activist, Panayote Dimitras, said of the Greek national myth: "Greek identity is constructed on the myth that every Greek speaks Greek and is Orthodox Christian by religion[.] These people [ethnic Macedonians] shatter that. By modern European and international human rights standards the way Greece treats them is condemnable."[640]

Yet, it is still unclear as to why Greek territorial aspirations on Macedonia included the borders of Macedonia under Phillip II, and not Macedonia's geographic borders any time before or after Phillip II.[641] Nevertheless, they picked those borders, and refer to Phillip the 2nd as Phillip the unifier rather than Phillip the barbarian and occupier, as history defines him.[642] In the early 1990s, when Macedonia was striving for independence and struggling for recognition, Greece wanted the world to believe that there was a Hellenic connection to ancient Macedonia.[643] Even today, the Greek Foreign Minister, Dora Bakoyannis, states that Aegean Macedonia "has had a Greek identity for more than three millennia,"[644] even though Aegean Macedonia was never a part of Greece until 1913. This is quite contrary to Greek actions of the first half of the 20th century, when after annexing it, Greece renamed Aegean Macedonia to 'Northern Greece' and destroyed the presence of

---

[633] Vangelov, Ognen, *The Greek Veto the Macedonian Identity*, 5.

[634] International Crisis Group, *Macedonia's Name: Breaking the Deadlock*, 3 (2009).

[635] Vangeli, Anastas, *Antiquity Musing: Reflections on the Greco-Macedonian Symbolic Contest over the Narratives of the Ancient Past*, 37 (2009).

[636] Agnew, John, *No Borders, No Nations: Making Greece in Macedonia*, 97 Annals of the Association of American Geographers 2, 2007: 406.

[637] *Id.*

[638] Sheridan, Dick, *Prof Cries Censorship*,
http://www.nydailynews.com/archives/ny_local/1996/02/09/1996-02-09_prof_cries_censorship.html Feb. 9th, 1996.

[639] Chirot, Daniel, *The Retribalization of the Modern World: How the Revival of Ancient Sentiments Leads to Persisting Nationalist and Ethnic Conflicts*, 14 (2008).

[640] Smith, Helena, *Bittersweet Return for Greek Civil War's Lost Victims: Greece is Allowing Ethnic Macedonians Exiled in the 1940s to Revisit Their Homes for the First Time*,
http://www.guardian.co.uk/world/2003/oct/17/greece . Oct. 17, 2003.

[641] Vangeli, Anastas, *Antiquity Musing: Reflections on the Greco-Macedonian Symbolic Contest over the Narratives of the Ancient Past*, 40 (2009).

[642] *Id.* at 41.

[643] Kofos, Evangelos, *Greece's Macedonian Adventure: The Controversy over FYROM's Independence and Recognition*, 3.

[644] *To Name or Not to Name? Greek Nationalism*, 3.

anything Macedonian and non-Greek.[645] Thus, "Greek hypersensitivity on Macedonia" and the associated dispute are mostly due to "the irksome challenge to modern Greece's own lineage to classical Greece[…]"[646]

Still, Greece wants the world to know about "the existence and identity of Greek Macedonia."[647] Yet, it does not want the world to remember how it occupied, annexed, and divided Macedonia; and it does not want the world to know about the policies it enacted to suppress the ethnic Macedonians who lived there, the actions used to deny any ethnic Macedonian connection to Aegean Macedonia, and how it virtually created a Greek-Macedonian identity through assimilation, expulsion and resettlement. As one Macedonian stated in reference to his home-region of Aegean Macedonia, "Greece does not trust the people who live here because they don't feel Greek – they don't speak Greek."[648]

However, it seems as if even some of the Greek people do not buy into this myth and know that their ethnic identity is not one rooted in ancient Greece. The Greek author of the book "Middlesex" explains:

> Being a modern Greek is immediately a comic situation because it's mock epic. You still believe that you've come from the ancient Greeks. There are all these arguments that the ancient Greeks were actually blond, that they were some Northern race that were inhabiting Greece. I know a little bit about things like that. Nevertheless, if you are born Greek-American, you do think that your heritage is Pericles and things like that. I remember being 8 years old and looking in the World Book and finding Alexander the Great and I said, "Dad, where's Macedonia?" and he said, "That's part of Greece." And I said, "We have him! We have Alexander the Great!"[649]

The modern Greek nation is based on ancient history and fabricated myths. This does not mean that there is no Greece or that there are no ethnic Greeks. However, it does suggest that ethnicity and identity are complicated concepts that cannot be defined by history, but only by the individual.

"Minority identity is a matter to be determined by the individual, and not by the state."[650] As Hugh Poulton put it, "[w]hat seems incontestable is that there are many Slavs in Yugoslavia, and… in Bulgaria and Greece and Albania, who live in the geographic area of Macedonia and who see themselves as Macedonian in identity."[651] Ethnic identity is a relatively new concept, especially in the Balkans. During the medieval times, "religion, family, and place played a much greater role than" ethnicity, and the term 'nation' referred to people who possessed certain legal privileges and not the culture or the language of the people.[652]

---

[645] Vangelov, Ognen, *The Greek Veto the Macedonian Identity*, 5.

[646] International Crisis Group, *Macedonia's Name: Why the Dispute Matters and How to Resolve It*, 14 (2001).

[647] International Crisis Group, *Macedonia's Name: Why the Dispute Matters and How to Resolve It*, 15 (2001).

[648] Gay McDougall Mission to Greece, *Promotion and Protection of All Human Rights, Civil, Political, Economic, Social and Cultural Rights, Including the Right to Development*, 14 (2009).

[649] *ET Sex, fate, and Zeus and Hera's Kinkiest Argument: "Middlesex" author Jeffrey Eugenides talks about hermaphrodites, ethnic assimilation, Detroit and whether men or women enjoy sex more.* Oct. 8, 2002.

[650] Human Rights Watch, *Denying Ethnic Identity: The Macedonians in Greece*, 18 (1994).

[651] Poulton, Hugh, *The Balkans: Minorities and States in Conflict*, 54 (1994).

[652] Rossos, Andrew, *Macedonia and the Macedonians*, 22 (2008).

But the issue is really simpler than this. Macedonians live for Macedonia; being 'Macedonian' is the central identifying feature for all Macedonians. Without *Macedonia*, the Bulgarians are still Bulgarians. Without *Macedonia*, the Greeks are still Greeks. Without *Macedonia*, the Serbs are still Serbs. Without *Macedonia*, the Albanians are still Albanian. Without *Macedonia*, the Macedonians no longer exist. As for all the other nations and peoples of the world, "Greece does not depend on the name Macedonia as the exclusive signifier of the Greek identity."[653] Macedonia does depend on the name Macedonia as the exclusive signifier of Macedonian identity. Thus, if the world wants these negotiations to fail, it will continue to let Greece deny Macedonians their right to declare and form their own identity.

2. Alexander the Great and Ancient Macedonia

Some believe that the name dispute really "is more a conflict over competing claims to the past - of who owns the cultural heritage of Macedonia, stretching back to ancient times."[654] Of course, this is only one aspect of a much more intricate and complicated issue. Still, the debate over entitlement to Alexander the Great and ancient Macedonia has been a source of pride and political empowerment for both Greece and Macedonia. Thus, it is not difficult to comprehend how this identity issue has caused both Macedonians and Greeks to incorporate the ancient past in this debate.

Alexander the Great was a mass murderer, and thus it could be a surprise that both Greece and Macedonia are so obsessed with him.[655] Alexander had fantasies of global conquest, declared himself a god, suppressed other religions, massacred much of his loyal staff, and betrayed his countrymen by hiring Persians, the former enemy, to supplant his infantry.[656] Yet, both ethnic Macedonians and ethnic Greeks have transformed him into a central part of their modern identities. Greece even imprisoned people who claimed the foregoing 'negative' attributes of Alexander, as it did when it convicted seventeen year old Michail Papadakis in 1992 of inciting divisions among people by distributing a leaflet which stated that "...Alexander the Great: War Criminal. Macedonia belongs to its people. There are no races; we are all of mixed descent."[657] As Michael Seraphinoff puts it:

> Both Macedonia and Greece would like to extend their roots back to include ancient glory. Both modern societies, however, bear no more real relation to the ancient societies that once existed on their soil than Italians bear to the ancient Romans, or modern Israelis to the ancient Hebrews, or modern Egyptians to the ancient Egyptians.[658]

One of the main differences, however, is that Greece tends to ignore everything that happened on Macedonian land during the 2000 years after Alexander's Macedonia

---

[653] International Crisis Group, *Macedonia's Name: Why the Dispute Matters and How to Resolve It*, 16 (2001).
[654] http://news.bbc.co.uk/2/hi/europe/1737425.stm .
[655] Vankin, Sam, *Gruevski's Macedonia, Greece, and Alexander the Great, History's Forgotten Madman*, (2009).
[656] *Id.*
[657] Human Rights Watch, *Denying Ethnic Identity: The Macedonians in Greece*, 25 (1994).
[658] Seraphinoff, Michael, *Dimensions of the Greek-Macedonian Name Dispute*, 3 (2008).

dissolved.[659]

Greece claims that they have the sole rights to the use of the name Macedonia because it suggests that the ancient territory of Macedonia was always Greek.[660] For example, the Greek Foreign Minister's letter to UN Secretary General Butros-Ghali suggested that a national flag with symbols from Greek history by Macedonia[661] was unacceptable to Greece. Macedonian President Gligorov responded to this assertion that it was not Macedonia's intention to steal Greek history.[662]

However, there is plenty of evidence that ancient Macedonian history is not really Greek history. Alexander the Great's soldiers would shout orders in Macedonian, not Greek.[663] Alexander and his Macedonians were identified as barbarians, which meant 'non-Greeks' in ancient Greek times,[664] and the Athenian philosopher Demosthenes continually outlined the distinction between Macedonian barbarianism and the superior culture of the Greeks.[665] It may be that "many [members of the] Macedonian elite may have talked like Greeks [and] dressed like Greeks, but they lived and acted like Macedonians, a people whose political and social system was alien to what most Greeks believed, wrote about, and practiced."[666]

The term 'Macedonian' was actually used interchangeably with the term 'enemy' in ancient Greek times.[667] The ancient writers often differentiated between Macedonia and the Greeks states, such as claiming that Macedonia's King Philip defeated the Greek states, or when Alexander's advisers urged him to "leave the Greek states to their own devices."[668] If ancient Macedonia was really a Greek state, these writers would have stated so. Further, ancient Greek writers would not write 'the Spartans were fighting the Greeks', or that the 'Athenians defeated the Greeks', because the Spartans and Athenians were Greeks. They did write that the Macedonians fought and defeated the Greeks because the Macedonians were not Greeks.

One author describes over a dozen references in modern Greek literature that describes ancient Macedonians as being a separate people than the ancient Greeks.[669] And while the ancient Macedonian language had Greek elements, its core was not Greek.[670] "It is clear that over a five-century span of writing in two languages representing a variety of historiographical and philosophical positions the ancient writers regarded the Greeks and Macedonians as two separate and distinct peoples whose relationship was marked by considerable antipathy, if not outright hostility."[671]

---

[659] Willi, Andreas. *Whose is Macedonia, Whose is Alexander?* The Classical Journal 105.1 (2009): 61..

[660] Underdown, Michael, *Background to the Macedonian Question*, 1 (1994).

[661] Apostolov, Mico, *The Macedonian Question -- Changes in Content Over Time*, x-xi (2006).

[662] *Id.* at xi.

[663] Underdown, Michael, *Background to the Macedonian Question*, 5 (1994).

[664] *Id.*

[665] Vangeli, Anastas, *Antiquity Musing: Reflections on the Greco-Macedonian Symbolic Contest over the Narratives of the Ancient Past*, 37 (2009).

[666] Rossos, Andrew, *Macedonia and the Macedonians*, 12 (2008).

[667] Vangeli, Anastas, *Antiquity Musing: Reflections on the Greco-Macedonian Symbolic Contest over the Narratives of the Ancient Past*, 7 (2009).

[668] Gergel, Tania, *Alexander the Great: Selected Texts from Arrian, Curtius and Plutarch.*

[669] Vangeli, Anastas, *Antiquity Musing: Reflections on the Greco-Macedonian Symbolic Contest over the Narratives of the Ancient Past*, 36 (2009).

[670] Underdown, Michael, *Background to the Macedonian Question*, 5 (1994).

[671] Seraphinoff, Michael, *Dimensions of the Greek-Macedonian Name Dispute*, 10 (2008).

John R. Knipfing wrote, in 1921, that King Philip of Ancient Macedonia combined "Greek with Macedonian virtues and vices."[672] This suggests that Greeks (which were comprised of citizens of several states) had different attributes and characteristics than Macedonians. Further, Knipfing writes that Philip was "rough only toward his uncivilized Macedonians, but considerate toward the culture-loving Greeks."[673] "He [King Philip] and his Macedonians […] succeeded in conquering the Hellenes because they understood and utilized the great principle of nationality."[674] Further, "the political and social life of the Macedonians had a basis so entirely different from that of the Greeks that Macedonia could never merge with Thebes and Athens to form a single state."[675] A 1957 article also explained the differences between ancient Macedonia and ancient Greece: "To the north of Ancient Greece was the country known as Macedonia. The people there were related to the Greeks, but had their own kingdom."[676] Even though the people may have been related somehow, ancient Macedonia was a separate and distinct entity from Greece. There are other examples, such as when Macedonia's Alexander I was to participate in Greece's Olympics, the Greeks protested, arguing that barbarians (non-Greeks) were not allowed to participate.[677] Furthermore, an Athenian statesman stated that King Philip was "… not only no Greek, nor related to the Greeks, but not even a barbarian from any place that can be named with honors, but a pestilent knave from Macedonia, whence it was never yet possible to buy a decent slave."[678]

In his 2011 book, *Alexander the Great*, Philip Freeman acknowledges that, without doubt, the ancient Macedonians did not view themselves as Greek, and the ancient Greeks did not view the ancient Macedonians as Greek.

> The Macedonian tongue was so far removed from the Greek of Athens or Sparta that it may as well have been a different language entirely. Years after his birth, when Alexander was in central Asia, he grew so angry at a drinking party one night that he switched from his usual Greek speech to yell at his guards in Macedonian. Later still his soldiers mocked an officer on trial for addressing them in Greek rather than the normal Macedonian of the ranks. Macedonians were known for their odd words and strange pronunciation – they could never quite get Greek sounds right even when they tried. Though their kings bore ancient Greek names, the Macedonian people called Philip *Bilippos* instead of the normal Greek *Philippos*. This only served to make them an object of further scorn to their pretentious critics in the Athenian assembly. Language, as well as politics, culture, and so much else, reinforced the opinion of the Greeks that the Macedonians were a separate people, barbarians from beyond Olympus, no matter how hard their kings might try to behave like Greeks. And to most Macedonians, this was just fine. They saw the Greeks as feeble, effeminate, self-important snobs who had long since squandered whatever manliness and courage they had possessed when they had driven back the Persian invaders more than a century earlier. The Macedonian nobility might study Greek philosophy and recite the poetry of Homer, but the common Macedonian soldier was proud not to be

---

[672] Knipfing, John R., *German Historians and Macedonian Imperialism* 26 The American Historical Review 4, Jul. 1921: 660
[673] *Id.* at 664.
[674] *Id.*
[675] *Id.*at. 666.
[676] *Macedonia*. The Pittsburgh Press. Oct. 27th, 1957: 113.
[677] *The Macedonian-Greek Conflict: The Age Long Conflict between the Greeks and the Macedonians*, http://www.historyofmacedonia.org/MacedonianGreekConflict/conflict.html
[678] *The Macedonian-Greek Conflict: The Age Long Conflict between the Greeks and the Macedonians*, http://www.historyofmacedonia.org/MacedonianGreekConflict/conflict.html

Greek.[679]

Could two peoples who live in such proximity to each other actually have been any more different?

The Greeks still point to evidence they think suggests the contrary. For example, part of the 'Oath of Alexander the Great' states: "I do not make discriminations between Greeks and barbarians as narrow-minded people do. [...] I will consider you all equal, white or black."[680] But this does not necessarily mean the barbarians, as the Macedonians were called, were necessarily 'ethnically' and 'culturally' similar to the Greeks. What it means is that Alexander had this vision of political and social unity, regardless of race, for the benefit of his Empire. This text does not scream 'Macedonians are Greeks'; it points out that some people, as they do today, push for a society that is blind to race and ethnicity when it concerns political and economic rights and status. This idea of Alexander the Great is rather something central to the ethnic Macedonian spirit, as when the Macedonian revolutionaries of the 1800s "intended to bring together – under the common denominator of 'Macedonian people'—members of different ethnic, confessional and national groups."[681] Of course, it is puzzling that Greeks point to this 'unity of ethnicities' quote by Alexander to prove his Greekness, as Greece is a state which denies the existence of ethnic minorities and rather believes that the right to exist "derives from the person's belonging to the dominant ethnic group and not from his/her participation in the political community, his/her payment of taxes to the State or his/her obedience to the Constitution of the country."[682]

Several other examples from Greece that claim ancient Macedonians were really Greek are disputed by Andreas Willi of the University of Oxford, which he did after examining a letter of 200 classical scholars to President Obama:

> The internet documentation which is referred to in the letter may be right when it sees nothing but "a personal grudge" behind Demosthenes' calling Philip II a "barbarian," but to cite Herodotus 5.22 as conclusive evidence that Alexander the Great was "thoroughly and indisputably Greek" is seriously misleading, since Herodotus' statement "I happen to know that [the forefathers of Alexander] are Greek" is triggered precisely by the existence of a dispute over the matter, long before the age of Demosthenes. As for (b), the question "Why was Greek the lingua franca all over Alexander's empire if he was a 'Macedonian'?" cannot be adequately answered with the words "[Because] Alexander the Great was Greek," given that we have numerous examples of ancient empires in which the lingua franca was not the language of the ruler. Nor can the presence of Heracles' head on Macedonian coins or Euripides' stay at the Macedonian court prove anything more than that the Macedonian kings were ready to embrace Greek traditions and Greek culture.[683]

Then there is the distinction between the ancient Greek and Macedonian languages, as one Western scholar on Slavic languages put it:

---

[679] Freeman, Philip, *Alexander the Great*, 5 (2011).
[680] Wieland, Carsten, *One Macedonia with Three Faces: Domestic Debates and Nation Concept*, 12.
[681] Marinov, Tchavdar, *We, the Macedonians: The Paths of Macedonian Supra-Nationalism (1878-1912)*, in *We, the People: Politics of National Peculiarity in Southeastern Europe* by Diana Mishkova, 109 (2009).
[682] *To Name or Not to Name?* Macedonia, 4.
[683] Willi, Andreas, *Whose is Macedonia, Whose is Alexander?* The Classical Journal 105.1 (2009): 59-60.

However, the ancient Macedonians were not Greeks and did not speak a Greek dialect, though they ultimately conquered Greece and, under Alexander the Great, carried Greek language and civilization to the entire eastern Mediterranean. The Macedonian language is recorded only in scanty glossary items compiled by the fifth-century Greek grammarian Hesychius. All that can be said about it with certainty is that it was Indo-European. It had some features that suggest close kinship with Greek and others that seem to link it to Illyrian, the ancestor of modern Albanian.[684]

Another commentator put a humorous twist on the Greek position regarding ancient Macedonia, stating that the Greeks idolize Alexander, but that he had a very different idea about name proliferation, leaving behind no less than ten Alexandrias in various parts of the world –one might imagine Alexander saying "[t]he more Macedonias, the better."[685] Even more humorous is Greece's recent wave of Macedonianizing its country. For example, the city in northern Greece, Thessaloniki, is named after Alexander's half-sister.[686] But Alexander never even knew of the city because it was "founded during the succession struggle that precipitated his death."[687] These examples show that Greece is not concerned so much as to what Alexander represented or about historical facts regarding Alexander's life and conquest; but rather Greece is concerned with ensuring that the Greeks have exclusive rights to him. Why should he not be shared by the world?

While ancient Macedonian and Greek history can give people pride, pleasure, and tourist dollars, the culture, genetics, and language of today's Macedonians and Greeks are significantly different than the ancients.[688] An overwhelming and unneeded focus on Alexander the Great and ancient Macedonia has allowed Greece to successfully turn this into a debate about a factual analysis of ancient history – an unwinnable debate as the few records we have from 2400 years ago will always be inconclusive. Consequently, the Macedonians have been tricked into centralizing their arguments and efforts with an ancient past to which they have few, if any, cultural connections. The question is not whether today's ethnic Macedonians are people with historical, cultural and ancestral ties to ancient Macedonians; the question is whether modern ethnic Macedonians have a right to determine for themselves their cultural and historical bonds, their own ethnic affiliation, and their own sense of identity. The answer to that question can only be 'yes'.

3. Foreign Influence

Foreign influence and intermingling is not only related to the present day events surrounding the Macedonian name dispute – there is a long history of international intervention in the Balkans. The foreign influence described in this section is presented in two forms. First, there is intervention by foreign national governments and international organizations. Some of this influence is directly related to achieving a solution to the

---

[684] Herman, Louis J., *History Doesn't Aid Greek Land Claim.*
http://select.nytimes.com/gst/abstract.html?res=F20617FD3C5A0C768CDDA80894D9494D81 . Jan. 5th, 1991.
[685] *The Two Macedonias*, The Albany Herald, April 11, 1992. Pg. 3,
[686] Mazower, Mark, *Salonica: City of Ghosts, Christians, Muslims, and Jews*, 1430-1950. 19 (2004).
[687] *Id.*
[688] Seraphinoff, Michael, *Dimensions of the Greek-Macedonian Name Dispute*, 3 (2008).

dispute; some of it is aimed at securing national self-interests. Second, there is influence from both the Macedonian and Greek Diasporas. In both forms the influence has at times drastically shifted the sentiment of the countries and the direction of their policies.

Influence from the international community

The Balkan countries are notorious for intermingling with the affairs of another country once they sense weakness. Once Macedonia became independent, Greece claimed it was afraid that Turkey and Bulgaria would come to Macedonia's aid in a political or military fight against Greece.[689] Historically, Greece has not been friends with either Turkey or Bulgaria. With Turkey, Greece disdain dates to Ottoman rule and the current Cyprus issue, along with minority issues. Greece feels that a close Macedonian alliance with Turkey poses a territorial threat.[690] As a matter of fact, Turkish President Turgut Ozal stated that Turkey was "the guardian of Macedonia."[691] Turkey also officially stated that the recent wave of NATO enlargement will not be complete until Macedonia is a member.[692] These statements were perceived as threatening by Greece,[693] although they were defensive and protective statements, not offensive to anyone.

However, the influence by neighboring Balkan nations is outdone by the pressure exerted by major world powers. The EU (and its predecessor, the EC) interfered significantly in the name dispute. The EC "delay[ed] recognition to Macedonia in order to save the Mitsotakis government from falling" in 1992, as Greek "Prime Minister Mitsotakis was an advocate of the Maastricht Treaty.[694] Thus, Mitsotakis' signature of the Maastricht Treaty guaranteed the development of the EU, and therefore the EC delayed recognizing Macedonia.[695] Mitsotakis also supported economic sanctions against Serbia in return for a delayed recognition.[696] In the late 1980s, Greece was in favor of preserving Yugoslavia, which brought her at odds with Germany, Italy, and Austria, who were in favor of Yugoslavia's dissolution.[697] This may have been because of the Macedonian issue, or the Macedonian issue may have been used as a bargaining chip with the greater powers. But as one European diplomat stated: "The Greeks are being totally ridiculous about this, and the only reason we haven't pressured them harder on it is that we're afraid of undercutting Mitsotakis and getting Papandreou again. The Greeks cause enough trouble in the community already, and we certainly don't need Papandreou."[698] Still, George H.W. Bush's appreciation for Greek Prime Minister Mitsotaki's other international actions also influenced the way the United States influenced the dispute. Mitsotakis had "consummated a controversial naval base agreement with the U.S.[,] [...] recognized

---

[689] Floudas, Demetrius A., *Pardon? A Conflict for a Name?: Fyrom's Dispute with Greece Revisited*, 6.
[690] Vangeli, Anastas, *Antiquity Musing: Reflections on the Greco-Macedonian Symbolic Contest over the Narratives of the Ancient Past*, 55 (2009).
[691] Thayer, Bradley. *Macedonia*, 133.
[692] *Assessing the Security Implications of Balkan Integration*. 18 (2009).
[693] Thayer, Bradley. *Macedonia*. 133.
[694] Paquin, Jonathan, *Managing Controversy: U.S. Stability Seeking and the Birth of the Macedonian State*, 444 (2008).
[695] *Id.*
[696] *Id.*
[697] Floudas, Demetrius A., *Pardon? A Conflict for a Name?: Fyrom's Dispute with Greece Revisited*, 9.
[698] Jack R. Payton, *"Europe Losing Patience with Greece's hard line on Macedonia." St. Petersburg Times.* Dec. 16, 1992.

Israel, […] [and] delivered Greek help for the war against Iraq"[699] in the early 1990s. This surely contributed to the US stance on the dispute.

There are those in the EU who currently insist on no Western interference in the negotiations, at least not directly. Eduard Kukan, an European Parliament member, stated that while the EU wants to see Macedonia in the EU and "in the European family," European involvement in the negotiations and mediation would make the name issue more complicated.[700] Further, some countries may even be displaying problematic obstacles to a quick and workable solution, giving Greece less incentive to compromise fairly, as evidenced by France and Greece's increased military contract negotiations.[701] Then there are those who believe influence is important. For example, "an appeal from [United Kingdom] FM Miliband to Greek FM Bakoyannis at the March 29 EU Gymnich, had failed to shift Athens off its hard-line position."[702] This irritated the position in the UK: "The UK's view is that now that Macedonia has accepted a compromise name proposed by UN Envoy Nimetz, maximum pressure must be brought to bear on the Greeks."[703] A Czech official also stated that it is "the EU's duty is to try to help find a solution as quickly as possible…"[704] This is important for Macedonia because Macedonia has "fulfilled all conditions and [has] received a positive assessment from the EU for two years."[705] Macedonia is more than willing to accept comments from the Czech official, who believes Greece's blockade of EU integration is not good.[706]

The US also had several reasons for recognizing Macedonia under its constitutional name, the Republic of Macedonia. The US did not want to recognize Macedonia in 2001 because it might have had the opposite effect of creating stability; not simply because a State Department official warned that this would anger the Greek-American community, but also because it may have negatively affected the outcome of the Albanian terrorist campaign in Macedonia.[707] Not only would the Albanians perceive the recognition as pro-Macedonian and anti-Albanian,[708] the possibility of another drastic Greek measure, like an embargo, could have jeopardized Macedonia in a time when it needed military, economic and political support, and could have sucked the whole region into a conflict. Some even argue that the reason that the US is so insistent on Macedonia joining NATO and the EU, and thus the reason for pushing a quick compromise on the Macedonian name and identity issue, is an energy 'power struggle' between the West and Russia. Macedonia

---

[699] Gelb, Leslie H., *Foreign Affairs; 'Macedonia' for Greece*,
http://select.nytimes.com/gst/abstract.html?res=F10613F93C5F0C718DDDAF0894DA494D81 Jun. 12th, 1992.
[700] *Kukan-Naumovski: Macedonia Belongs to the European Family*,
http://www.mia.com.mk/default.aspx?vId=81361516&lId=2 . February 21, 2011.
[701] *NATO Macedonia Invitation: UK Effort Fail to Move Athens*, Feb. 4, 2011.
http://www.telegraph.co.uk/news/wikileaks-files/london-wikileaks/8305009/NATO-MACEDONIA-INVIT
ATION-UK-EFFORTS-FAIL-TO-MOVE-ATHENS.html
[702] *Id.*
[703] *Id.*
[704] *Klaus: EU should interfere in Macedonian name dispute*, Feb 9, 2011.
http://praguemonitor.com/2011/02/09/klaus-eu-should-interfere-macedonian-name-dispute
[705] *Id.*
[706] *Id.*
[707] Paquin, Jonathan, *Managing Controversy: U.S. Stability Seeking and the Birth of the Macedonian State*, 453 (2008).
[708] *Id.*

is "bound up with European and American energy interests," and "major energy corridors either pass through [Macedonia] or are scheduled to pass through it, such as the AMBO oil pipeline or the Nabucco gas pipeline[...]"[709] Whatever reasons for interfering, foreign intervention has lefts its mark on the name dispute.

Diaspora influence.
Foreign influence also comes in the form of activities by the Greek and Macedonian Diasporas. As Loring Danforth describes:

> The 'global cultural war' between Greeks and Macedonians over which group has the right to identify itself as Macedonians involves not only the two Balkan states of Greece and Macedonia, but Greek and Macedonian diaspora communities in Europe, the United States, Canada and Australia as well. Political demonstrations in 1990-91 in Greece, the Re-public of Macedonia, western Europe, Canada and Australia; international conferences sponsored by Greek organizations like the Australian Institute of Macedonian Studies in Melbourne in 1988 and the Pan-Macedonian Association in Thessaloniki and New York in 1989; and the lobbying efforts of Macedonian groups such as the Macedonian Information and Liaison Service in Brussels, the International Macedonian Lobby and the Macedonian World Congress are the vehicles through which this transnational national conflict between Greeks and Macedonians is being waged.[710]

For example, a Greek group named "'Americans for the Just Resolution of the Macedonian Issue' [...] paid for two full-page advertisements in the *New York Times* ... against the recognition" of Macedonia as the Republic of Macedonia.[711] They framed Macedonia as having an extremist position and making claims on Greece's territory.[712]
In the early 2000s, the Greek Diaspora even took the name dispute and their claims to levels that even disturbed the Greek government:

> The Greek diaspora is so proud of Alexander the Great, [...] and so keen to establish him as Greek, that it wants to carve his effigy on a cliff face on Mount Kerdyllion. The Greek authorities in Athens are horrified, but the Alexander the Great Foundation, based in Chicago, is eager to get chipping, and says its members will cover the $45m cost. Grotesque as it may consider the scheme—the monument would be four times the size of the American presidents carved on Mount Rushmore—the Greek government may yield. It is to rich Greek-Americans that it turns when it wants to promote its interests in America.[713]

The Greek-Americans were so intent on winning this cultural war that they practically ignored the warnings by many Greek environmentalists and archaeologists of the dangerous implications. "Environmentalists fear[ed] it [would] spoil the landscape and harm the area, while archaeologists [...] called the project a 'monstrosity' that they [said] could threaten a nearby ancient theatre and a Byzantine church."[714] But as a Greek

---

[709] Kosanic, Zoran, *Obstacle's to FYROM's Membership of NATO: A Tougher Agenda Than Expected*, 5 (2009).
[710] Danforth, Loring, *Claims to Macedonian Identity: The Macedonian Question and the Breakup of Yugoslavia*. 9 Anthropology Today 4, Aug. 1993: 8.
[711] Paquin, Jonathan, *Managing Controversy: U.S. Stability Seeking and the Birth of the Macedonian State*, 446 (2008).
[712] *Id.*
[713] *A World of Exiles.* http://www.economist.com/node/1511765?story_id=1511765 . Jan. 2, 2003.
[714] *Alexander the Great Plan Sparks Row.* http://news.bbc.co.uk/2/hi/europe/2210108.stm . Aug. 22nd,

politician pointed out, "it doesn't matter if archaeologists say it's going to be just kitsch."[715] Thus, implementing outlandish behavior to destroy the Earth and the history of the land is okay when it is for purposes of denying ethnic Macedonians their identity. As one person pointed out (with regards to Greece's name dispute with Macedonia), "[t]he Former Yugoslav Republic of Macedonia could do the same thing, [...] [w]here would that lead?"[716]

The Greeks in America enjoyed "one of the most effective ethnic groups in Washington" during the 1990s, with this Greek-American lobby representing 3 million Greek-Americans.[717] Once President Clinton recognized the independence of Macedonia, Greek-Americans stepped up their lobbying efforts:

> Within a few days, the American Hellenic Educational Progressive Association collected 30,000 signatures against President Clinton's decision. Several leaders of the community, including Representative Michael Bilirakis of Florida and Senator Paul Sarbanes of Maryland, asked President Clinton to reverse his decision and managed to convince George Stephanopoulos to consult President Clinton about it. Members of a national Hellenic group also pressured the U.S. Congress "to urge that President Clinton rescind American recognition of the Republic of Macedonia," which led Congress to pass a resolution asking the president to reconsider its Decision.[718]

President Clinton did cave into some of these demands when he promised to not send an ambassador to Macedonia until Greece and Macedonia could solve the name and flag issue.[719] But the Greeks' efforts were not only limited to targeting the federal government. As Gregory Michaelidis writes:

> In 2002, chapters of a pro-Greek diaspora group, the Pan-Macedonian Association, which considers the Macedonian name to be part of Greek heritage, began lobbying U.S. state legislators to pass resolutions declaring "that the ancient Macedonians were Hellenes (or Greeks), and that the inhabitants of Macedonia today are their Hellenic descendants and part of the northern province of Greece, Macedonia." The resolutions passed in Missouri, California, Illinois, and other states with sizable Greek-American populations.[720]

The Greek lobby quickly infiltrated the governments of the US in order to strengthen the Greek position.

The Greek-American community eventually became very active in engaging the George W. Bush administration after Bush recognized Macedonia under its constitutional name in 2004. Bush did so one day after the US presidential elections, calculating that an earlier recognition would have isolated the Greek-American community and would have been politically costly.[721] Immediately, the Greek lobby demanded that the US reverse its

---

2002.

[715] *Id.*

[716] *Id.*

[717] Paquin, Jonathan, *Managing Controversy: U.S. Stability Seeking and the Birth of the Macedonian State*, 449 (2008).

[718] *Id.*

[719] *Id.* at 450.

[720] Michaelidis, Gregory, *Salvation Abroad: Macedonian Migration to North America and the Making of Modern Macedonia, 1870-1970*, 289 (2005).

[721] Paquin, Jonathan, *Managing Controversy: U.S. Stability Seeking and the Birth of the Macedonian State*, 453 (2008).

stance.[722] The Greek-American Archbishop first sent a letter demanding the U.S. revoke its recognition; then, a Greek-American delegation traveled to Washington, D.C. and held several meetings with top U.S. officials, including Secretary of State Colin Powell, National Security Advisor Condoleezza Rice, and Bush advisor Karl Rove.[723] But their efforts proved futile, as "Powell explained that the decision to recognize the name was irrevocable. ... 'We knew that the decision would create great pain to [the Greek-American community] but we had no choice. The objective was to reinforce stability in Macedonia.'" [724] Further attempts by the Greek-American community to persuade Congress also failed.[725] In 2005, the Greek-American community took their efforts to the US Congress. The Hellenic Caucus group of Congress tabled a resolution "calling on the [f]ormer Yugoslav Republic of Macedonia (FYROM) to put an end to its negative and nationalistic propaganda against Greece and to cooperate with the United Nations and Athens to find a mutually acceptable name to the land-locked republic[.]"[726] Although not as intensive today, the Greek lobby continues to infiltrate local and state governments regarding the name dispute.

To the contrary, the campaign by Macedonian-Americans to gain US recognition of Macedonia's independence in the early 1990s consisted mostly of letter writing,[727] demonstrations, phone calls and the occasional meetings with politicians in Washington, D.C.[728] The most effective earliest Macedonian organization was the MPO, or the Macedonian Patriotic Organization.[729] The MPO had been involved in Macedonian issues for several decades before Macedonia's independence. Actually, in 1962, the MPO initiated a campaign to reunite Macedonia and make it an independent nation, similar to Switzerland,[730] which had been suggested at the turn of the century many times. The MPO's recommendations went as follows, according to the article:

> The MPO recommends as a first step the three divided parts of Macedonia be placed temporarily under the protectorate of the United Nations. 'We are certain that the people in Macedonia will cooperate fully with [the] United Nations Commission.' At the end of a few years, when the U.N. Commission decides the proper time has come, the MPO suggests a free plebiscite under U.N. supervision to determine the future organization of an independent Macedonia with equal rights and equal obligations for all its inhabitants. 'We believe this to be the only solution and [a] just solution of the Macedonian question and urge all men of peace and good will to help us to attain [it.]'[731]

Those efforts, however, were not successful. Today, Macedonian-Americans have developed and are developing many successful political associations, such as the United

---

[722] *Id.* at 454.
[723] *Id.*
[724] *Id.*
[725] *Id.* at 454-55.
[726] *US Draft Resolution Urges FYROM to Stop Propaganda Against Greece.* http://www.greeknewsonline.com/?p=3977 . Oct. 31st, 2005.
[727] Paquin, Jonathan, *Managing Controversy: U.S. Stability Seeking and the Birth of the Macedonian State*, 449 (2008).
[728] *Id.*
[729] *Id.*
[730] *Macedonians Make Bid for Independence: U.S. Group Meets in Buffalo, Recommends UN Cooperation.* Youngstown Vindicator. Sept. 9th, 1962: 11.
[731] *Id.*

Macedonian Diaspora.

Groups in Canada and Australia are also very proactive and abundant. In Australia, for example, there are over 300,000 Greeks and 200,000 Macedonians.[732] The Greeks in Australia are quite a powerful political and economic force. As Greek-Australian Illias Rallis stated: "[w]e have power. We can use it on the behalf of Greece."[733] As a matter of fact, as reported in 2003, "Macedonia has no embassy in Australia because Greeks think the former Yugoslav republic that calls itself Macedonia has purloined the name from them, and the Greek vote counts for a lot in Australia. [...] [T]he Australian government has not yet allowed it [Macedonia] to open an embassy in Canberra."[734] The Greek influence in all sectors of Australian society was almost insurmountable during the early stages of the name dispute, with the Australian media constantly acknowledging pro-Greek rallies and demonstrations while completely ignoring massive Macedonian protests and demonstrations.[735]

Thus, in Australia, the Macedonia community had to be on the defensive,[736] defending their existence: "Macedonia has a long and proud history and has been instrumental in the development of European culture, yet Greeks say we don't exist. I exist, I am here, I am flesh and blood," said Kiril Jonovski of the Illawarra Macedonian Lobby Group.[737] Even in January of 1988, the Australian Diocese of the Macedonian Orthodox Church put a quarter-page advertisement in an Australian newspaper, *The Age*, defending its Macedonian identity.[738] In the advertisement, the Macedonians talked about how a Greek sponsored congress, called the 'International Congress of Macedonian Studies,' had the aims of denying the existence "of the Macedonian people, its culture, language and history[.]"[739] They believed the Congress's purpose was to negate the Macedonians, "Hellenize the Macedonian community," and "inflame anti-Macedonian propaganda."[740]

Three other prominent groups of the 1990s were the 'Macedonian Council of Australia', the 'Aegean Macedonian Association of Australia'[741] and the 'Macedonian Human Rights Committee'.[742] In 1993, the Aegean Macedonian Association of Australia sent an extensive letter to the Human Rights Subcommittee of the Australian Parliament's Joint Standing Committee on Foreign Affairs, Defense and Trade.[743] AMAA's letter explained the history of human rights abuses in Greece, and then made recommendations for the Greek government in addressing these problems, and how Australia could use its

---

[732] Shea, John, *Macedonia and Greece: The Struggle to Define a New Nation*, 187.

[733] *Id.* at 189.

[734] *A World of Exiles.* http://www.economist.com/node/1511765?story_id=1511765 . Jan. 2, 2003.

[735] Warne, Leslie, *We Exist, Say Illawarra Macedonians*, http://www.greenleft.org.au/node/2031 Mar. 11th, 1992.

[736] Shea, John, *Macedonia and Greece: The Struggle to Define a New Nation*, 189.

[737] Warne, Leslie, *We Exist, Say Illawarra Macedonians*, http://www.greenleft.org.au/node/2031 Mar. 11th, 1992.

[738] *The Macedonians: Statement of the Macedonian Community in Australia.* The Age. Feb. 2nd, 1988: 3.

[739] *Id.*

[740] *Id.*

[741] Shea, John, *Macedonia and Greece: The Struggle to Define a New Nation*, 189.

[742] Warne, Leslie, *We Exist, Say Illawarra Macedonians*, http://www.greenleft.org.au/node/2031 Mar. 11th, 1992.

[743] *The Human Rights Situation of Macedonians in Greece and Australia*, http://www.pollitecon.com/html/life/The_Human_Rights_Situation_of_Macedonians_in_Greece_and_Australia.html . Jul. 1993.

influence and standing to help achieve this. [744] They furthermore highlighted the discrimination against Macedonians in Australia, by highlighting how a television broadcasting company aired over 150 hours of Greek language programming a year while only airing just under three hours of Macedonian language programming a year. [745] They even asked for Australia to gather "credible statistics on the number of Macedonians in Australia, something it cannot do at present despite having had credible figures on other nationalities for many decades," and asked for ethnic Macedonians who come from Greece to be counted as ethnic Macedonians and not as ethnic Greeks. [746] On one occasion "an Australian judge of Macedonian background confronted Greek government officials over the proper definition of national identity which should apply in the dispute over the human rights of the Macedonian minority in northern Greece." [747]

The Macedonia Diaspora has also been surprisingly good at uniting their efforts. An excellent example is when Macedonians from the United States, Germany and Sweden collaborated to register not only the 'macedonia.eu' domain along with other variants of Macedonia, but also the 'greece.eu' domain and other variants. Slave Saveski's and Boris Andonovski's actions are both explained in a 2005 article:

> "The same day when ".eu" top-level domain was launched, I received an e-mail message from a friend of mine living in USA and owning the "vmacedonia.com" address. He said: "Slave, get it immediately, to be ours, Macedonian." I did that and apart from "macedonia.eu" I have also applied for "makedonija.eu" and for "grece.eu"," said Saveski in his letter to Vreme.
> [...]
> "Most of the web addresses registered with the name Macedonia are owned by organisations or individuals from Greece. They publish contents that deny our existence and because of that I applied for the "greece.eu" address. If EURid grants me the address I will publish content about Macedonia in Macedonian," said Andonovski. [748]

However, Greece did the same thing, requesting to register 'macedonia.edu.' [749] Still, it shows how the Diaspora can come together to influence the ongoing saga of Greek denial of the Macedonian identity. This is also highlighted by the Association of Macedonians in Poland's effort to collaborate with Macedonians in Australia to publish a book that the group wrote discussing Greece's human rights atrocities on its Macedonian minority. [750]

Thus, it has been demonstrated that international influence with regards to the Macedonian name dispute comes in many forms and for many reasons. Although it is difficult to assess the direct effects this interference has had on the positions of both Macedonia and Greece, it has become clear that this dispute extends well beyond the borders of Macedonia and Greece, rendering it difficult for a solution to be reached.

---

[744] Id.
[745] Id.
[746] Id.
[747] Danforth, Loring, *Claims to Macedonian Identity: The Macedonian Question and the Breakup of Yugoslavia.* 9 Anthropology Today 4 Aug. 1993: 9.
[748] Nikoloski, Vladimir, *Macedonians Living Abroad Defend Macedonia on the Internet.* http://www.metamorphosis.org.mk/en/news/old-articles/580 . Dec. 20th, 2005.
[749] Id.
[750] *The Human Rights Situation of Macedonians in Greece and Australia,* http://www.pollitecon.com/html/life/The_Human_Rights_Situation_of_Macedonians_in_Greece_and_Aust ralia.html . Jul. 1993.

4. Internal Politics

Greece cannot continue under a climate of underhand dealings and the undermining of the Government's work. The people govern Greece, not backstage dealings and shady interests.[751]

Greece and the Greeks have always played politics with the Macedonian Question to benefit their interests within the Greek government and society. For example, a look back to the Greek Civil War of the 1940s highlights how the Greek communists played politics to advance their positions:

> [T]he Greek communist leadership chose to manipulate the Macedonian question to further its own party interests. Whenever the KKE needed the political and military support of the Macedonians, it paid lip service to their demands and made some half-hearted concessions to them without giving up control over them or their movement. When the KKE no longer felt in need of their support, it turned against them, canceled the concessions, and downplayed their demands and the Macedonian problem in Greece.[752]

As Tenko Maleski, the Macedonian Foreign Minister during the early 1990s, declared: Greek "politicians have been playing with the patriotic emotions of their people."[753]

However, internal political maneuvering also affects Macedonia, albeit to a lesser extent. For example, Macedonian elections will be held soon, in June of 2011. Depending on how he reacts to Greece's positions and actions, Prime Minister Gruevski could end up facing a regime change.[754] Actually, regime changes have happened several times in the past in both Macedonia and Greece. Thus, it is in Gruevski's interest to center his political platform around national pride during a time when the Macedonia has been burned by Greece and the international community.

Earlier, in 2001, when a poll of Macedonians sought to seek Macedonians' reactions to a potential Macedonia compromise with Greece that would change its name, 80% of Macedonians would have demanded a regime change had that happened.[755] Hence, Macedonia's Prime Minister at the time, Georgievski, who once suggested that a compromise would work if Macedonia got money and aid from Greece, had to back down from that position.[756] Macedonians escaped having a politician sell their identity through utilizing the threat of possible regime change.

Some believe the current Macedonian ruling political party has misused the dispute to intensify nationalistic slogans.[757] To some extent, this may be true for certain

---

[751] *Greek Chief Calls Election after Losing Majority.*
http://select.nytimes.com/gst/abstract.html?res=F00611FF395B0C738DDDA00894DB494D81 . Sep. 10th, 1993. Quote by Constantine Mitsotakis

[752] Rossos, Andrew, *Incompatible Allies: Greek Communism and Macedonian Nationalism in the Civil War in Greece, 1943-1949*, 69 The Journal of Modern History 1, 1997: 48.

[753] Fotiadis, Apostolis, *A Country Is In a Name.* http://www.ipsnews.net/news.asp?idnews=39782 . Oct. 24th, 2007.

[754] Vankin, Sam, The *Republic of North Macedonia and Palestine: Obama Loses Patience With Bush Allies.* June 3, 2009.

[755] Tziampiris, Aristotle, *The Name Dispute in the Former Yugoslav Republic of Macedonia After the Signing of the Interim Accord*, 240.

[756] *Id.* at 241.

[757] *Assessing the Security Implications of Balkan Integration.* 12 (2009).

politicians. However, if one examines the issue closely enough, the Greek veto is actually the cause of the recent political complications in Macedonia: it was part of the Greek strategy.[758] Immediately after the veto, VMRO-DPMNE, Macedonia's ruling party, and DUI, the main ethnic Albanian opposition party, "call[ed] for snap elections ... instead of forging a united front...."[759] Instead of allying with DUI, Prime Minister Gruevski stated that he would rather ally with the smaller ethnic Albanian party, DPA, and DUI then threatened to force federalization of Macedonia if the Albanian party with the most votes was not part of the next government coalition.[760] This tension escalated on voting day, when over 30 polling stations, primarily in Albanian dominated areas, experienced violence, "while major irregularities and ballot manipulation [affected] almost 50 percent of the Albanian vote, or 10 percent of the total electorate in the country."[761] Therefore, although assuming a 'nationalistic tone' may have personal benefits for certain politicians, it also coincides with the desires of the Macedonian people, especially after destabilizing events perpetrated by Greece. Still, some of these nationalist overtones may create future obstacles for the stability of Macedonia.

The two leaders of Greece and Macedonia in 1995 were also not willing to sacrifice their political image at home for a compromise.[762] As a matter of fact, this has been true for many Macedonian politicians throughout the past two decades. As the former Macedonian Prime Minister Branko Crvenkovski stated: "this matter [of the name] is important for the national identity of my country [...] some in my country might take a pro-Greek position, but I would like to know who – regardless of their rank – could announce something like that to the people."[763] It is difficult for a politician to survive without incorporating patriotism in their platform.

Yet, the name issue is provocative enough in Greece to bring down a government.[764] Therefore it makes sense that even moderate Greek politicians are not willing to risk a political future by conceding any of their positions. Recently, Greece's Foreign Minister, Dimitris Droustas, said that the opposition leader "Samaras should not sacrifice national interests for the sake of partisan support and wondered where was the current opposition leader when the United States recognized Macedonia under the constitutional name."[765] Of course, with over 80% of Greek citizens desiring a Greece veto of Macedonia's accession into NATO, as demonstrated by a February 2008 poll, it would have been politically damaging to do otherwise.[766] However, when polled whether citizens supported a veto of Macedonia into NATO as the 'former Yugoslav Republic of Macedonia,' which would be illegal if Greece did so, only three-fifths of Greek citizens

---

[758] Matovski, Aleksandar, *Macedonia After Bucharest: Avoiding Another European Failure in the Balkans.* 3 (2008).

[759] *Id.*

[760] *Id.*

[761] *Id.*

[762] Kondonis, Haralambos, *Bilateral Relations Between Greece and the Former Yugoslav Republic of Macedonia,* 58.

[763] Kostovilis, Spyridon, *Exploring the Sources of Greek Foreign Policy Towards the Former Yugoslav Republic of Macedonia,* 21 (2005).

[764] International Crisis Group, *Macedonia's Name: Breaking the Deadlock,* 6 (2009).

[765] "*Greek PM Pessimistic on Name Solution.*" http://macedoniaonline.eu/content/view/17448/2/ Jan. 25, 2011

[766] Seraphinoff, Michael, *Dimensions of the Greek-Macedonian Name Dispute,* 2 (2008).

supported such veto.[767] Even though that is a significantly lower number of people, it is still more than half of the population and it would have been politically costly for a leader to accept Macedonia's accession under that name.

Similar political divisions highlighted Greek politics throughout the early 1990s. During that time, "[t]he name issue had become a burning political issue in Greece and the option of supporting Macedonia's recognition was politically untenable."[768] "[A]ny hint by the Greek government that it could accept a designation including the term 'Macedonia' was bound to be viewed domestically as a capitulation," and thus "…Greek public opinion served as a constrain[t] limiting the [Prime Minister's] room for diplomatic maneuvering."[769] Greece's Foreign Minister in the early 1990s, Andonis Samaras, was trying to get the Europeans to accept the maximalist Greek position, while Greek Prime Minister Mitsotakis was also approaching his European colleagues, except with a more willingness to compromise.[770] In fashionable Balkan politics, Mitsotakis then dismissed Samaras from his position, reversed his own stance and then began promoting the maximalist views.[771] He apparently did this because most of Greece's party leaders endorsed the maximalist approach, and accepting the maximalist line would score him political and internal points and neutralize his main opponent, Andreas Papandreou.[772] Still, Samaras and others demanded Greece use more forceful methods in denying Macedonia its name.[773] The political struggles continued, as Kofos puts it:

> "Mitsotakis … was presented by UN mediators Vance and Owen with the compromise version of a draft treaty covering all outstanding questions between Athens and Skopje, including the issue of the name. Despite the fact that his government—with Michalis Papaconstantinou, an experienced and moderate politician and native of Greek [Aegean] Macedonia, as the new foreign minister—had given signs early in 1993 of departing from the maximalist line, and being ready to discuss a compound name, Mitsotakis retreated at the last moment. This time, a number of influential MPs of his party, including Miltiadis Evert, presented him with a quasi-ultimatum not to proceed with signing the proposed draft. Otherwise, they "for[e]cast", the government would lose its parliamentary majority and would be forced to resign. The prime minister succumbed and ordered Papaconstantinou to return to Athens.[774]

Eventually, in September of 1993, the aforementioned internal misfortunes of Greece, along with some other developments, brought down the Greek government.[775] Mitsotakis

[767] *Greek Diplomat Summoned Home Over Macedonia Comments.*
http://www.forbes.com/feeds/afx/2007/07/06/afx3888877.html . Jun. 7th, 2007.
[768] Paquin, Jonathan, *Managing Controversy: U.S. Stability Seeking and the Birth of the Macedonian State*, 444 (2008).
[769] Kostovilis, Spyridon, *Exploring the Sources of Greek Foreign Policy Towards the Former Yugoslav Republic of Macedonia*, 21 (2005).
[770] Kofos, Evangelos, *Greece's Macedonian Adventure: The Controversy over FYROM's Independence and Recognition*, 7.
[771] *Id.*
[772] *Id.*
[773] *Greek Chief Calls Election after Losing Majority.*
http://select.nytimes.com/gst/abstract.html?res=F00611FF395B0C738DDDA00894DB494D81 . Sep. 10th, 1993.
[774] Kofos, Evangelos, *Greece's Macedonian Adventure: The Controversy over FYROM's Independence and Recognition*, 7.
[775] *Id.*

dissolved Parliament and early elections were held.[776] Once the Papandreou regime was in place, talks with Macedonia were immediately suspended.[777]

The nature of these political maneuverings has shifted Greece's 'red line' in regards to what they are willing to compromise about. In 2010, the Greek Foreign Minister stated that "there is absolutely no chance of the neighbouring country's accession to NATO with the so-called constitutional name 'Republic of Macedonia'."[778] This is contrary to the position of Greece in 2006, when it did not object to term Macedonia being in the 'Republic of Macedonia's' name, and accepted that Macedonia did not have territorial claims, and thus shifted the argument to be about Greek heritage, historical sensitivity, and cultural identity.[779] Greece also came out with the position stating that a red line is that geographical Macedonia cannot be considered Macedonians' homeland.[780] As the Macedonian Vice Prime Minister said in February, 2011:

> It has become a practice [for] Greek politicians to repeat a so called "red line" i.e. a name for overall use with geographical determinant. They can repeat their "red line" a hundred times and we'll reiterate a thousand times that the Republic of Macedonia will never accept blackmail and that times when others made crucial decisions for Macedonians and all citizens living on this territory without taking them into consideration have long passed[.][781]

But the real reason Greece has so many red lines may be because it is simply trying to avoid meaningful negotiation – Greek politicians are "reluctant to accept any compromise solution, since this would be seen as defeat."[782] This adversarial and deceptive approach is explored in the next section.

5. Greece's Adversarial Approach to Compromising

Greece is employing bully tactics. It's a terrible precedent to set – one country imposing a name on another.[783]

[776] *Greek Chief Calls Election after Losing Majority.*
http://select.nytimes.com/gst/abstract.html?res=F00611FF395B0C738DDDA00894DB494D81 . Sep. 10th, 1993.
[777] *Greece Losing on Policy Over 'Macedonia.'*
http://select.nytimes.com/gst/abstract.html?res=F00612FF3A580C758EDDA90994DB494D81 Oct. 26th, 1993.
[778] *FM outlines foreign policy to Greek ambassadors*
http://www.ana.gr/anaweb/user/showplain?maindoc=5571641&maindocimg=5435499&service=10 Sep, 12, 2010.
[779] Axt, Heinz-Jurgen et. al., *The Greek Macedonian Name Dispute -- Reconciliation through Europeanization?*, 26 (2006).
[780] Kofos, Evangelos, *The Current Macedonian Issue between Athens and Skopje: Is there an Option for a Breakthrough?* 3 (2009).
[781] *Kukan-Naumovski: Macedonia Belongs to the European Family,*
http://www.mia.com.mk/default.aspx?vId=81361516&lId=2 . February 21, 2011
[782] *Macedonia: New Developments in Name Row With Greece.* www.rferl.org/content/article/1058423.html . Apr. 13th, 2005.
[783] *Macedonia is Denied Recognition.* The Rochester Sentinel, August 15th, 1992: 1. Quote by Janusz Bugajski.

My main aim was to convince the Republic (of Macedonia) to declare that there is no Slavomacedonian minority in Greece. This was the real key of our difference with Skopje.[784]

Greece has had an inflexible position throughout much of the negotiations.[785] Because Greece was far superior economically, politically, and militarily than Macedonia throughout the 1990s, other nations viewed this as Greece being a bully.[786] Greek actions, such as a near-total "unconscionable"[787] embargo on goods coming from and going to Macedonia, "made its mark on international perceptions as proof that Greece's Macedonian policy was bullying and aggressive."[788] Jacques Delors, the former President of the EC, even labeled Greece as the "sick man of Europe" because of its negative actions and reactions.[789] Not only was Greece causing problems for Macedonia, but Denmark's 1993 Foreign Minister, Uffe Ellemann-Jensen, stated that Greece was "holding the EC hostage and fail[ed] to act in the Community spirit by refusing to recognize Macedonia as a sovereign state."[790]

Undeniably, Greece has been "less inclined to compromise,"[791] as evidenced by "one Greek diplomat comment[ing], 'We will choke Skopje into submission.'"[792] Essentially, Greece became greedy and started demanding too much. As one senior Greek official stated, "[w]e have reached a nationalistic delirium."[793] And as Jack R. Payton of the St. Petersburg times declared: "Your [the Greeks] partners in the European Community are getting totally fed up with you. Some are even wondering why they let Greece join the community in the first place."[794] It was a perception by many, and still is by some, that Greece had become an unhealthy and destabilizing force in Europe.

In addition to imposing devastating embargoes against Macedonia in 1995, Greece tried preventing other countries from normalizing relations with Macedonia.[795] From the onset of Macedonia's independence from Yugoslavia, Greece was initially successful in

---

[784] *MHRMI Urges Sanctions Against Greece, Immediate Recognition of Macedonia.* Quote by former Greek Prime Minister, Constantine Mitsotakis, http://www.mhrmi.org/news/2008/april03b_e.asp . April 3rd, 2008.
[785] Floudas, Demetrius A., *Pardon? A Conflict for a Name?: Fyrom's Dispute with Greece Revisited,* 9.
[786] *Id.*
[787] International Crisis Group, *Macedonia's Name: Why the Dispute Matters and How to Resolve It,* 17 (2001).
[788] Kofos, Evangelos, *Greece's Macedonian Adventure: The Controversy over FYROM's Independence and Recognition,* 9.
[789] Axt, Heinz-Jurgen et. al., *The Greek Macedonian Name Dispute -- Reconciliation through Europeanization?,* 15 (2006).
[790] Lambert, Sarah, *Greek Refusal to Recognise Macedonia Comes Under Fire.* http://www.independent.co.uk/news/world/europe/greek-refusal-to-recognise-macedonia-comes-under-fire-1479801.html . Jan. 21st, 1993.
[791] Kosanic, Zoran, *Obstacle's to FYROM's Membership of NATO: A Tougher Agenda Than Expected,* 4 (2009).
[792] Rossos, Andrew, *Macedonia and the Macedonians,* 270 (2008).
[793] Simons, Marlise, *For the Name of Macedonia, a Burst of Greek Pride,* http://select.nytimes.com/gst/abstract.html?res=F10615FA3C5E0C748DDDAD0894DA494D81 Apr. 17, 1992.
[794] Jack R. Payton, *"Europe Losing Patience with Greece's hard line on Macedonia." St. Petersburg Times.* Dec. 16, 1992.
[795] Acevska, Ljubica, *The Republic of Macedonia: An Atypical Balkan Country.* 1997. 20 Fordham Int'l L.J. 1521, 1528.

this campaign by lying to the EC.[796] For example, Greece insisted to these countries that Tito recreated the name Macedonia in the 1940s, and deemphasized the importance of Macedonia to the Macedonians.[797] More recently, Greece vetoed Macedonia's accession into NATO solely over its name, even though Macedonia "made incredible strides since its independence in 1991, achieving membership in the United Nations, the Organization for Security and Cooperation in Europe, the World Trade Organization, and to NATO's Partnership for Peace and Membership Action Plan," as Peter Welch, a Congressman from Vermont, read into the Congressional Record in February 2008.[798] Congressman Welch hoped that Macedonia would have been invited into NATO at the Bucharest Summit in April of that year.[799] The Macedonian Army has been working with the Vermont National Guard since 1995, with many joint efforts aimed at preparing the Macedonian Army for its uncertain NATO accession date.[800] Still, in 2009, Greece even "threatened Iceland's EU bid because its ambassador to the US planned to screen a documentary about Macedonia's pursuit of recognition under its constitutional name."[801] As former US Secretary of State, Lawrence Eagleburger asked. "Is there anything more immature and more foolish than 'blackmailing' a nation by denying its membership in international organizations…[?]"[802]

In the months leading up to the veto on Macedonia's accession into NATO, Greece intensified its veto threats against Macedonia. The Greek Foreign Minister, Dora Bakoyannis said, "[w]e should make it clear that we are now at a turning point where Skopje could receive an invitation to join NATO. It is time for decisions[.]"[803] Macedonia rejected this aggression: "Macedonia is using the force of arguments, while Greece is trying to use the argument of force, which is not a good message."[804] According to the US Undersecretary of State R. Nicholas Burns, speaking a few years before Greece's veto of Macedonia into NATO, "it would be a 'shame' if Greece used its veto power[.]"[805]

Some argue that Macedonia is also playing a game of avoidance. Sam Vankin suggests that Prime Minister Gruevski of Macedonia is more concerned about economic growth and nation building than he is about handling the name issue.[806] Yet, both Macedonia and Greece are trying to avoid negotiations, because each country's negotiators hope that by playing for time, they will "obtain the best possible advantages from a future agreement."[807] For example, because the Albanian situation in Macedonia could lead to a

---

[796] Schteppan, Hans L., *Comedy: Greek By Name*. http://maknews.com/html/articles/stefov/stefov121.html . February, 2008.

[797] *Id.*

[798] Seraphinoff, Michael, *Dimensions of the Greek-Macedonian Name Dispute*, 8 (2008).

[799] *Id.*

[800] Welch, Peter, *Celebrating Vermont's Partnership with the Republic of Macedonia*. Congressional Record – Extension of Remarks. E176. Feb. 13th, 2008. http://umdiaspora.org/images/Vermont.pdf .

[801] *MHRMI Condemns Latest Greek Tactic in Name Dispute with Macedonia.* http://www.mhrmi.org/news/2009/november23_e.asp . Nov. 23rd, 2009.

[802] *Eagleburger: Greece Has No Historic Right to Dispute Over Macedonia's Name.* http://macedoniadaily.blogspot.com/2010/09/eagleburger-greece-has-no-historic.html

[803] *Macedonia Foreign Minister Rebuffs Greek Threats.* http://www.balkaninsight.com/en/article/macedonia-foreign-minister-rebuffs-greek-threats . Oct. 15th, 2007.

[804] *Id.*

[805] *Bush Praises Macedonia's Implementation of Peace Agreement.* http://newsblaze.com/story/20051027085523nnnn.nb/topstory.html . Oct. 27th, 2005.

[806] Vankin, Sam. *Macedonians in Denial about the Name Issue Dispute With Greece.* June 5, 2009.

[807] Kosanic, Zoran, *Obstacle's to FYROM's Membership of NATO: A Tougher Agenda Than Expected.* 3

partition of Macedonia, Greece has less incentive to stabilize a country that may have a limited future.[808] The logic may be that Macedonia would be more likely to compromise when it is experiencing instability. But some Greeks may believe the opposite – they believe that the name issue does not or will not create major instability in Macedonia or for Macedonians,[809] and thus they can delay the negotiations.

Greece has more incentive to not find a solution by avoiding the negotiations, however. "While Greece is Macedonia's third biggest trading partner," Macedonia does not even occupy a position on "Greece's top dozen largest trading partner list."[810] In addition to Greece holding veto power over Macedonia's EU accession, this factor leads many Greeks to believe that Macedonia needs Greece.[811] It has been a tactic of Greece to emphasize the economic benefits while playing down Macedonia's identity claim. Greek Ambassador Adamantios Vassilakis hinted at this when he stated in 2007 "that the economic cooperation between them is more valuable than other theoretical positions[.]"[812] It has been repeatedly stated and repeatedly confirmed that Greece is "prepared to use economic dependency as a pressure tool."[813] The 2007 Greek Deputy Foreign Minister, Theodoros Kassimis, iterated: "Greece does not want to economically strangle (FYROM)… but we are following this policy so they realize that the restoration of smooth ethnic tensions will be significant for their growth."[814] In other words, Greece is telling Macedonians what their primary interests should be, by suggesting that money is more valuable than identity.

Yet, Macedonia may not need Greece as much as Greece would like to think, such as is indicated when Macedonia claims it will not bow to Greek pressure to change its identity. "If Macedonia has to choose between it constitutional name and NATO accession, we say in advance that we choose the first," said former President Branko Crvnekovski.[815] "The changing of Macedonia's constitutional name, at Greece's request, would be too high a price to pay for the country's NATO membership," echoed Prime Minister Gruevski.[816]

Another tactic Greece utilizes has been to shift the starting point of the name negotiations. In the early 1990s Greece objected so adamantly that negotiations led to an interim agreement, with the UN recognizing Macedonia as the 'former Yugoslav Republic of Macedonia'. Now, Greece does not want to start from the name 'Republic of Macedonia' as a basis to hold negotiations, which was Macedonia's original position, but rather from the 'former Yugoslav Republic of Macedonia'. They argue this despite the fact that the UN Interim Accord was a temporary solution, designating the 'former Yugoslav

---

(2009).

[808] International Crisis Group, *Macedonia's Name: Why the Dispute Matters and How to Resolve It*, 14 (2001).

[809] *Id.*

[810] *Id.*

[811] *Id.*

[812] *U.N. Hands Greece and Macedonia Name Proposals.* http://uk.reuters.com/article/2007/11/01/uk-greece-macedonia-un-idUKN0146056820071101 . Nov. 1st, 2007.

[813] Fotiadis, Apostolis. *A Country Is In a Name.* http://www.ipsnews.net/news.asp?idnews=39782 . Oct. 24th, 2007.

[814] *Id.*

[815] *Macedonia "No" to Trading Its Name.* http://www.balkaninsight.com/en/article/macedonia-no-to-trading-its-name . Nov. 5th, 2007.

[816] *Id..*

Republic of Macedonia' as a provisional name until the parties could agree to the name.[817] Similarly, when Nimetz proposed 'Republic of Macedonia-Skopje' in 2005, Greek Foreign Minister Petros Molyviatis stated that the name suggestion "did not totally satisfy Greece, but it was a basis for negotiations which Greece is ready to partake in a positive and constructive spirit."[818] Thus, Greece has been wittingly successful in shifting Macedonia's beginning negotiating stance in order to meet in a 'middle' that is actually closer to Greece's desired outcome.

But it is not just a name game; it is also a blame game. Greek Ambassador Thrasyvoulos Terry Stamatopoulos said Greece is committed to the UN process of mediation and that it has made significant compromises, adding that Macedonia should do the same.[819] Further, the Greek Foreign Minister stated in September of 2010 that Macedonia should "abandon actions and practices of irredentist propaganda and … actively show that it is following a policy of good neighbourliness."[820] Greece has even been harsher, when in April of 2010 the Greek Foreign Minister stated that Greece was willing to unblock Macedonia's accession into the EU if it accepts 'North Macedonia' as a name, and that Macedonian Prime Minister Gruevski would "have to explain to his people why he is depriving them of their European prospects."[821] Not only is Greece trying to convince the world that Macedonia is at fault for the standstill in negotiations, but Greece is trying to convince the Macedonian people that Macedonia is at fault.

Greece blamed Macedonia for stealing Greece's cultural and historical symbols, such as when Macedonia adopted the 16-ray Vergina sun as its flag, to which Greece immediately objected.[822] Yet, Greece did not adopt this as the flag for Aegean Macedonia until after Macedonia did.[823] Greece even attempted a propaganda campaign blaming Macedonians for stealing Greece's culture, such as when its embassy in London accused Macedonia of printing currency with pictures of the 'White Tower of Salonika', a place in Aegean Macedonia.[824] Macedonian officials showed international reporters all of the new printed currency, of which none contained this symbol.[825] Greece has yet to accuse other countries of stealing Greek history, even when neighboring Bulgaria built a huge statue of Alexander the Great,[826] and the US has a city named Alexandria[827] and several cities named 'Macedonia', such as in Iowa, Illinois, and Ohio. In reality, what Greece is forcing Macedonia to do is to "surrender their history, tradition, and culture, which [are] all

---

[817] *Id.*

[818] *Greece Considers Macedonia Name.* http://news.bbc.co.uk/2/hi/europe/4425249.stm . Apr. 8th, 2005.

[819] *Assessing the Security Implications of Balkan Integration.* 7 (2009).

[820] *FM outlines foreign policy to Greek ambassadors*
http://www.ana.gr/anaweb/user/showplain?maindoc=5571641&maindocimg=5435499&service=10 Sep, 12, 2010.

[821] *Report: Greece OK with New Macedonian Name,*
http://www.upi.com/Top_News/World-News/2010/04/06/Report-Greece-OK-with-new-Macedonia-name/UPI-87691270559245/ April 6, 2010.

[822] Vangelov, Ognen, *The Greek Veto the Macedonian Identity*, 6.

[823] *Id.*

[824] Savill, Annika. *Macedonians Warn of War.*
http://www.independent.co.uk/news/world/europe/macedonians-warn-of-war-1533124.html . Jul. 14th, 1992.

[825] *Id.*

[826] Frye, Timothy. *Macedonia and EU Integration: Deputy Prime Minister of Macedonia Vasko Naumovski.* 1 (2010).

[827] *Id.*

inseparable from their national name," which they have had for 3,500 years.[828]

Although Greece blamed Macedonia for the frightening implications Macedonia's constitution contained for interference in Greek internal affairs, its accusations amounted to a massive exaggeration. The 1992 Macedonian constitution stated that it "care[d] for the status and the rights" of ethnic Macedonian minorities in other countries.[829] It further stated that it would assist these Macedonians in cultural development and promote ties to them.[830] Certainly, states should not forcefully interfere in another's affairs. However, Greece overly exaggerated and overemphasized the traumatizing implications, as it did when it sensationalized the threat an independent Macedonia would pose, by holding huge demonstrations that was based on the theme that 'Macedonia is Greek,' and by political parties creating platforms requiring Macedonia to drop both its name and flag.[831] Further, in the early 1990s, Greece almost placed an embargo on Albania for its treatment of the ethnic Greek minority in Albania.[832] Therefore, it seems as if this hypocritical argument by Greece accusing Macedonia of wanting Greek territory because its constitution promotes cultural ties and cares about minority rights pales in severity to Greece's intentions to inject itself into another nation's minority problems. The truth is that Greece does not want to recognize that a Macedonian minority exists within its borders; and another state legally acknowledging that a Macedonian minority exists in Greece poses as an obstacle to this desire.[833]

The adversity is not limited to Macedonia and Greece; ethnic tensions have flared up throughout the world where significant communities of Macedonians and Greeks reside. Australia has seen some violence and a lot of tension between Greeks and Macedonians.[834] For example, in Australia, after world recognition of Macedonia as an independent country in 1994, Greeks bombed, burned and destroyed many Macedonian properties, including churches.[835] Even in 1988, Macedonian protestors, demanding that Greece grant Aegean Macedonia autonomy, were throwing eggs at a limousine driving Greece's President Christo Sartzetakis to a meeting in Sydney, and one Macedonian was charged with assault.[836] Similar sentiments, with less violence, have also consumed the US and Canada.

With regards to NATO accession, there is a general agreement among NATO leaders that Macedonian had fulfilled requirements to join NATO;[837] yet Greece still blocks Macedonia's efforts. Perhaps Greece is using NATO for an upper-hand in the name issue; or perhaps Greece is using the name issue to block Macedonian accession into NATO and the EU.[838] Either way, Greece is being an "obstructionist partner" by bringing

---

[828] Rossos, Andrew, *Macedonia and the Macedonians*, 269 (2008).

[829] Thayer, Bradley. *Macedonia*. 132.

[830] *Id.*

[831] International Crisis Group, *Macedonia's Name: Why the Dispute Matters and How to Resolve It*, 13 (2001).

[832] Vankin, Sam. *Greeks Bearing Gifts – Greek Investments in the Balkans.* http://www.globalpolitician.com/print.asp?id=1135

[833] Thayer, Bradley. *Macedonia*. 132.

[834] Underdown, Michael, *Background to the Macedonian Question*, 10 (1994).

[835] Shea, John, *Macedonia and Greece: The Struggle to Define a New Nation*, 188.

[836] *Youth Shot in Ethnic Demonstration; Macedonians Assail Greek President.* The News and Courier. Nov. 28th, 1988.

[837] *Assessing the Security Implications of Balkan Integration.* 12 (2009).

[838] *NATO Macedonia Invitation: UK Effort Fail to Move Athens*, Feb. 4, 2011.

"bilateral disputes into the Alliance," which works against the principles of NATO.[839] This only angers the Macedonians, and as one Macedonian foreign minister warned, "[i]f they [the Greeks] knew this behavior would cost them, they might change their opinion."[840]

Greece blocked Macedonia's accession into NATO, as it did when it prevented the world from recognizing Macedonia's independence, with the justification that Macedonia poses a security risk to Greece's territorial integrity. However, there are major disparities in size, military capabilities, and geopolitical and economic power between the two countries.[841] Macedonia does not have the ability to claim any part of Greece.[842] As Ljubica Acevska explained when Greece was vehemently making these accusations during Macedonia's quest for independence: "It's unrealistic to think that we [Macedonia] could invade. Greece is larger, more powerful, a member of NATO. We're undeveloped. We're just forming our own army. We don't have any weapons."[843] This is not to suggest that Macedonians in Greece might not one day rebel against Greek authorities for abuses against them, as the Macedonians did after World War II. However, this is not akin to Macedonia invading Greece and attempting to carve up Greek territory.

It is true that some Macedonians have territorial claims to parts of Greece,[844] as parts of Greece were stolen from Macedonia in the early 20th century. In the early 1990s, as a reaction to Greece's strong objection to an independent Macedonia, the VMRO-DPMNE political party of Macedonia "pledged to work for the 'ideal of all free Macedonians united' in a Macedonian state."[845] They sold maps which depicted Solun (Thessaloniki) as the capitol of this free Macedonia, and they claimed symbolic connections to Alexander the Great.[846] The Macedonian Deputy Speaker of Parliament even stated that Greece "has no legitimate right over Aegean Macedonia."[847] However, this dangerous attitude, whether founded on truth or not, is common among factions in all Balkan nations. There are elements in Greece who have territorial claims on southern Albania.[848] Many Albanians have claims on Macedonia, Greece, Montenegro, and Serbia, in addition to a near-complete expulsion of the Serbs out of Kosovo. Bulgarian factions have desires for parts of Greece, Macedonia, and Serbia. Certain Serbs believe land in Bulgaria, Croatia and Bosnia is rightfully Serbian, in addition to wanting Kosovo back. Further, Croats have the same thoughts on Bosnia and Serbia. Thus, the claim that some Macedonians want to reunite the people on land that was annexed by Greece in 1913 is not an indication of one nation's hostilities toward another; it is a reflection of the sentiment of tragedy that has plagued the Macedonians for several centuries. This struggle for survival and preservation

---

http://www.telegraph.co.uk/news/wikileaks-files/london-wikileaks/8305009/NATO-MACEDONIA-INVIT ATION-UK-EFFORTS-FAIL-TO-MOVE-ATHENS.html

[839] McNamara, Sally and Morgan L. Roach, *The Obama Administration Must Push for Macedonia's Accession to NATO at the Lisbon Summit*, The Heritage Foundation. Web Memo No. 3037, 1 (2010).

[840] http://www.idividi.com.mk/English/440126/index.html . May 7th, 2008.

[841] Vankin, Sam. The *Republic of North Macedonia and Palestine: Obama Loses Patience With Bush Allies.* June 3, 2009.

[842] Underdown, Michael, *Background to the Macedonian Question*, 8 (1994).

[843] *Macedonia is Denied Recognition.* The Rochester Sentinel, August 15th, 1992: 1.

[844] Underdown, Michael, *Background to the Macedonian Question*, 7 (1994).

[845] International Crisis Group, *Macedonia's Name: Why the Dispute Matters and How to Resolve It*, 13 (2001).

[846] *Id.*

[847] Thayer, Bradley. *Macedonia*. 133.

[848] Underdown, Michael, *Background to the Macedonian Question*, 7 (1994).

of national identity and territorial integrity contributed to nationalistic attitudes in Macedonia during the 1990s.[849] The nationalism was a reaction to Greece's policy against Macedonia and Macedonians.

Greece has used, and will use, any argument to justify avoiding the main underlying issues of the dispute, even when the risks to peace and stability are severe. As the Danish Foreign Minister put it in the early 1990s:

> Here you have a very small country with problems of immense magnitude that has managed to keep a fragile balance between the nationalities and has maintained a coalition government that groups the very factions fighting each other elsewhere [...] I fear we might see a second Sarajevo develop there if we cannot give [the Macedonians] our support.[850]

Still, Greece insisted that "[t]his pseudo little republic must stop irritating us."[851] Because according to Greek MEP Eleni Maria Koppa, how could Greece be to blame when Macedonia "ha[d] not met the Copenhagen criteria over media freedom [and] judiciary independence[?]"[852] Thus, the Greek argument is: "how can Macedonia have the right to self-determination when the country still needs judicial and media reforms?" The Greeks have not only added unrelated arguments and conditions to the name dispute, but are setting illegal and unethical standards for self-determination that other countries in the international community may eventually look to in relations with other countries. These political choices have made Greece part of the problem.[853]

Further, in February 2011, spokesperson Gregory Delavekouras for the Greek foreign ministry actually placed the blame on the Macedonians, stating:

> "Greece has shown – and Greece has shown this at the negotiating table – that we want to move ahead to a solution and we want to do it now. The leadership of the Former Yugoslav Republic of Macedonia – which has on the one hand stated that it wants a solution, but has essentially remained stationary – needs to take the necessary steps so that we can reach a solution."[854]

Just a month earlier, the Greek Prime Minister, George Papandreou, told Greek MPs that Macedonians are refusing to compromise, and yet that Greece will not waiver from its position:

> "I am not an optimist over the prospects for swift settlement of the name dispute with fyr Macedonia. The other side refuses to accept a name with geographical qualifier for all uses. The Greek positions and initiatives in the issue are stable and constant. We will not stop in our efforts to find a mutually acceptable solution. We have a national strategy and

---

[849] Kondonis, Haralambos, *Bilateral Relations Between Greece and the Former Yugoslav Republic of Macedonia*, 56.

[850] Lambert, Sarah, *Greek Refusal to Recognise Macedonia Comes Under Fire.* http://www.independent.co.uk/news/world/europe/greek-refusal-to-recognise-macedonia-comes-under-fire-1479801.html . Jan. 21st, 1993.

[851] *The Two Macedonias,* The Albany Herald, April 11, 1992: 3.

[852] *"Macedonia to start EU accession negotiations, reads EP draft-resolution"* Feb. 10, 2011 .http://macedoniaonline.eu/content/view/17544/45/

[853] Kondonis, Haralambos, *Bilateral Relations Between Greece and the Former Yugoslav Republic of Macedonia*, 56.

[854] *Greece- MFA - Briefing of diplomatic correspondence by Foreign Ministry spokesman Gregory Delavekouras*, 9 February 2011 http://www.isria.com/pages/10_February_2011_187.php

clearly drawn red lines."[855]

It seems as if a red line for Greece is that whatever name Macedonia accepts, it has to be for all uses, including its constitutional and domestic use.

Certainly, Macedonia has its redline, and after several years of compromising on its UN name, flag and constitution in order to free itself from the grip of a devastating embargo, Macedonia feels as if it has compromised enough with regards to Macedonia's standing internationally. As the Macedonian Ambassador, Nikola Dimitrov, stated: "[w]e are very flexible when it comes to bilateral communication with Greece, but we have to maintain the position that [...] we have a right for a constitutional name, to be used internationally."[856] The former Macedonian Prime Minister, Vlado Buckovski, issued a statement in 2005 that has been Macedonia's consistent and resounding red line: "The double formula is on the table. We think that is a greater compromise than the compromise Greece is trying to come up with."[857] In essence, Macedonia should not have to negotiate with anyone over its name. But it is willing to accept a bilateral name that is acceptable to Greece.

Still, Macedonia is not quiet in returning the blame. PM Gruevski stated that "Greece feels no pressure at all to solve the name row [and]… is neither worried at all nor motivated to make a compromise."[858] This may or may not be true. But still, "[t]he Greek position implies a *superior* – often *exclusive* – right to the contemporary appellation as well as the ancient heritage of Macedonia."[859] How can Macedonia expect Greece to want to compromise with this attitude?

Greece's adversarial nature has not just been aimed at the Republic of Macedonia throughout the negotiation process. In late 1993, the Greek Deputy Foreign Minister, Theodoros Pangalos, made a statement attacking Germany: "Before, Germany was a giant with clay feet, and now it is like Pantagruel, the giant of Rabelais, with a bestial force and a child's brain[.]"[860] He said this in reference to German desires to "hurry along diplomatic relations" with Macedonia, and that Germany was approaching an age of pan-Germansim that Europe experienced between World War I and World War II.[861] He made these remarks even when it is "[a] basic tenet of EU membership" to "never publicly insult a partner country."[862] Further, in 1992, because Greece was so aggressively opposed to the term 'Macedonia' appearing in the newly independent country's name, Greece "threatened to close its northern border in retaliation and paralyze an important international transit

---

[855] *"Greek PM Pessimistic on Name Solution."* http://macedoniaonline.eu/content/view/17448/2/ Jan. 25, 2011

[856] *U.N. Hands Greece and Macedonia Name Proposals.* http://uk.reuters.com/article/2007/11/01/uk-greece-macedonia-un-idUKN0146056820071101 . Nov. 1st, 2007.

[857] *Greece Considers Macedonia Name.* http://news.bbc.co.uk/2/hi/europe/4425249.stm . Apr. 8th, 2005.

[858] *PM Gruevski: I wish a name solution with Greece to be found,* January 19, 2011 http://www.focus-fen.net/index.php?id=n239881

[859] International Crisis Group, *Macedonia's Name: Why the Dispute Matters and How to Resolve It,* 16 (2001).

[860] Doyle, Leonard. *Greek Outburst Enrages Germans.* http://www.independent.co.uk/news/greek-outburst-enrages-germans-1506948.html . Nov. 27th, 1993.

[861] *Id.*

[862] *Id..*

route" if Europe kept on ignoring its demands.[863] Not only did Greece threaten Macedonia, it threatened the economy and security of the continent.

The adversarial positions that Greece has assumed and the unproductive attitude it has displayed throughout the past two decades have dragged the dispute into territory that it should have never ventured into. Greece's actions have amounted to "a long campaign […] to isolate the tiny Balkan country of Macedonia until it changes its name[.]"[864] These actions do not align with fair negotiations and discussions, and one wonders if Greece will ever be willing to seek a solution based on good faith.

6. What about the Name?

The name Macedonia was not always an issue for Greece. Actually, "[b]efore the collapse of Communist Yugoslavia, Greece accepted the existence of a Yugoslav republic named Macedonia."[865] Still, throughout this dispute, not only has Greece been "heatedly proclaiming that the name Macedonia is exclusively Greek," Greece claims "that it has been theirs for 3,000 years[.]"[866] Thus, to avoid calling the Republic of Macedonia by the name 'Macedonia', Greece has advocated and currently calls Macedonia 'Skopje' and 'FRYOM,'[867] among other names.

For Macedonians (as it is for everyone in the world), the choice of a name is a basic human right; it is their existence.[868] As Macedonia's Foreign Affairs Minister, Antonio Milososki, said in 2008, "[t]he name Macedonia is the foundation of the Macedonian identity. With it we're not posing a threat to anyone and we're not taking anything from anyone."[869] Former President Kiril Gligorov stated that complying with Greek demands of a name change would also mean that the Macedonian people would lose their ethnic name.[870] Further, according to international law, every nation has a sovereign right to use its constitutional name.[871] Yet, Greece feels that Macedonia's refusal to change its constitutional name is an inflexible position.[872] But any Macedonian government that

---

[863] Simons, Marlise, *For the Name of Macedonia, a Burst of Greek Pride,*
http://select.nytimes.com/gst/abstract.html?res=F10615FA3C5E0C748DDDAD0894DA494D81 Apr. 17, 1992..

[864] Lewis, Paul. *Europe to Defy Greece on Ties to Macedonia.*
http://select.nytimes.com/gst/abstract.html?res=F00616F83A5A0C718DDDAB0994DB494D81 Dec. 12th, 1993.

[865] *Greece Losing on Policy Over 'Macedonia.'*
http://select.nytimes.com/gst/abstract.html?res=F00612FF3A580C758EDDA90994DB494D81 Oct. 26th, 1993.

[866] Simons, Marlise, *For the Name of Macedonia, a Burst of Greek Pride,*
http://select.nytimes.com/gst/abstract.html?res=F10615FA3C5E0C748DDDAD0894DA494D81 Apr. 17, 1992.

[867]*Macedonia: New Developments in Name Row With Greece.* www.rferl.org/content/article/1058423.html .
Apr. 13th, 2005.

[868] International Crisis Group, *Macedonia's Name: Breaking the Deadlock,* 3 (2009).

[869] Kosanic, Zoran, *Obstacle's to FYROM's Membership of NATO: A Tougher Agenda Than Expected,* 1 (2009).

[870] Rossos, Andrew, *Macedonia and the Macedonians,* 269 (2008).

[871] Axt, Heinz-Jurgen et. al., *The Greek Macedonian Name Dispute -- Reconciliation through Europeanization?,* 26 (2006).

[872] *Id.*

changes Macedonia's name will be accused of treason.[873]

One analysis gives four strong arguments suggesting that a change of Macedonia's name amounts to an eventual elimination of the Macedonian identity. First, "the name at once identifies the state and the people[.]"[874] For example, if the name of Macedonia is changed to the 'Republic of Vardar', the people will not be thought of as Macedonians but as Vardarians (or something similar). Second, Bulgaria is currently challenging the Macedonian identity.[875] Any change in Macedonia's name will legally confirm Bulgaria's accusations that Macedonians are really not their own people, and thus provoke more Bulgarian ambitions to advocate a position that the people of 'Macedonia' are really Bulgarians. Third, "the provisional name the 'former Yugoslav Republic of Macedonia' is not only a humiliation, but implies a provisional acceptance of the state[.]"[876] If the name dispute continues, or if Macedonia's name is changed, Macedonia will be prevented from achieving the goals of a wealthy and prosperous country for its people. Finally, after the concessions Macedonia made with regards to the OhridAagreement with ethnic Albanians, Macedonia has no room to concede on their identity.[877] In the Balkans, countries are maintained through a strong legal, political, cultural and religious presence of one ethnic group. With the successful implementation of the Ohrid Agreement, Macedonia has been the most progressive nation with regards to creating a peaceful and workable multi-ethnic state. A change in Macedonia's name will heighten Macedonian fears that the Macedonian nation and identity will soon be eliminated

Even though the name of Macedonia is painted by the media and world as the central issue between Greece and Macedonia, it is actually the newest aspect of the debate, and probably even a strategic distraction to other issues, such as identity, territory control, resource control, and history:

> "...[D]uring the long and turbulent development of the "Macedonian Question" (1870-1945-1991) all involved parties struggled against each other about everything, but never struggled about the name of Macedonia. In the 19th century the rival Greek and Bulgarian Church contend over the Macedonian dioceses and Christian believers; later on the Internal Macedonian Revolutionary Organization (IMRO) fought against the Ottomans and the Greeks aiming to create an independent Macedonian state; during the Balkan and the World Wars young Greek, Bulgarian and Serbian monarchies fought and allied among themselves to occupy larger part of geographic territory of Macedonia and control the region; during the Tito's Yugoslavia, with the Socialist Republic of Macedonia being one of its six republics, quarreled with Greece over the rights of the unrecognized Macedonian minority and the Greek Civil War refugees; during the Cold War historians and linguists from Athens and Thessalonica crossed swords with their colleagues from Skopje over national languages, Macedonian ethnic identity, and antique and modern history. But, until the dissolution of Yugoslavia and constitution of the independent Republic of Macedonia (1991-92) no one had ever, nor bilaterally neither internationally, disputed the name Macedonia as such."[878]

---

[873] *To Name or Not to Name? Greek Nationalism Ltd.*, 6.

[874] International Crisis Group, *Macedonia's Name: Why the Dispute Matters and How to Resolve It*, 15 (2001).

[875] *Id.*

[876] *Id.*

[877] *Id.*

[878] Axt, Heinz-Jurgen et. al., *The Greek Macedonian Name Dispute -- Reconciliation through Europeanization?*, 8 (2006).

Still, Greece has now created the objection to Macedonia's name based on the belief that only Greece can use the name Macedonia.[879] President Gligorov once tried to appease the Greeks by offering to call the new nation the 'Repbulic Macedonia-Skopje', but Greece rejected this offer by saying the use of Macedonia in any form or combination was unacceptable. [880] Although the root problems are not about the name, Greece has successfully turned into a problem about a name.

Yet, if we focus solely on the name issue, the fact that there is a province called Macedonia in Greece holds no real significance to the Republic of Macedonia's name, even when we put aside the fact that the 'Republic of Macedonia' was called the 'People's Republic of Macedonia' before northern Greece was renamed to Macedonia in the late 1980s. For example, there is a province in Belgium called Luxembourg, but there is also a country called Luxembourg.[881] These two nations have maintained peace and economic prosperity without jeopardizing one another's future. Of course, the histories of the countries' relations are not the same. But when focusing only on the aspect of who is entitled to the rights to the name 'Macedonia', Greece's fears of the Republic of Macedonia's use of the name 'Macedonia' seems unjustified and unsupported by history.

Furthermore, Greece has not responded fairly or collaboratively to reasonable name solutions. For example, Greece rejected the name 'Republika Makedonija' for use in international organizations offered by Nimetz.[882] It rejected this proposal, first officially suggested in 2002, even though it could still call the internationally recognized 'Republika Makedonija' whatever it wanted.[883] Moreover, the unrealistic demands of Greece regarding the name, however, reach levels of lunacy when Greece insists that Macedonia not only change its name for use within international organizations, bur that Macedonia changes its name for all uses, meaning Macedonia would have to change its name in its own constitution.[884] This demand conflicts with the Preamble of the Interim Accord the two countries signed in 1995, which states that the countries should not "intervene…in any form, in the internal affairs of the other,"[885] and with Article 3, which states that each party must "respect…the political independence of the other party."[886] If how the Macedonian people decide to define themselves in their own constitution is vulnerable in the negotiation process, Macedonia may have no choice but to consider the interim accord meaningless and begin interference with minority issues in Greece.

Some Greeks have further advocated the use of the name 'Vardarska Banovina' for the Republic of Macedonia because they say it is historically justified. Today's portion of geographic Macedonian territory is labeled as such on a few maps. As a 2008 UMD letter to Secretary of State Condoleezza Rice emphasized:

> "Vardarska Banovina" is not a proper name for the Republic of Macedonia's territory. This term was instituted during the reign of Serbian King Alexander I in the

---

[879] *The Two Macedonias,* The Albany Herald, April 11, 1992: 3.
[880] Jack R. Payton, *"Europe Losing Patience with Greece's hard line on Macedonia." St. Petersburg Times.* Dec. 16, 1992.
[881] Underdown, Michael, *Background to the Macedonian Question,* 12 (1994).
[882] International Crisis Group, *Macedonia's Name: Breaking the Deadlock,* 5 (2009).
[883] http://news.bbc.co.uk/2/hi/europe/1737425.stm .
[884] Taleski, Dane, *Macedonia After the Greek Veto for Membership in NATO: Analysis of the Effects and the Situation.* April, 2008: 1.
[885] *Id.*
[886] *Id.* at 2.

1929 administrative reorganization of the Kingdom of Serbs, Croats, and Slovenes. This reorganization changed 33 "oblasts" (provinces) into 9 "banovinas," all named after rivers and geographic features, of the newly-named "Kingdom of Yugoslavia." If Macedonia is "Vardarska Banovina," then Croatia is "Sava Banovina," and Slovenia is "Drava Banovina," as they were called then.[887]

Thus, not only has this proposed name never been used to identify a country or a people, it is based on one king's administrative regime that the people of that time had no legitimate say in implementing. How does this coincide with self-determination?

Another issue that Greeks have with Macedonia calling itself Macedonia is that, because the Republic of Macedonia does not cover the entire geographic Macedonia, the name 'Republic of Macedonia' will allow the republic to monopolize everything Macedonian, and thus destabilize the region.[888] Yet, Macedonians insist that they do not want their claim to Macedonia to be exhaustive.[889] Macedonians have only suggested that Macedonia has the right to self-determination. Greece has its own right to self-determination, and may name itself and its provinces whatever it likes without objection from Macedonia or any other nation. For the name 'Macedonia', it is possible for two countries to both utilize the same name without conflicts. Macedonians point to the name 'United States of America' and how just because the US utilizes the name 'America', this does not necessarily mean that it stakes claim to all South American and North American history, or that it has territorial ambitions toward any other 'American' nation.[890] As the Deputy Prime Minister of Macedonia, Vasko Naumovski, put it: "Imagine if Canada told the United States of America to change its name because America spans beyond U.S."[891] Should the US be forced to change its name?

While the name is only a symptom of the tension between Greece and the existence of the Macedonian people, the implications for any change in the name will have devastating consequences for the existence of the Macedonian people. Still, Greece continues its untenable stance on the Macedonian name issue by continually belittling the significance of the value of Macedonia's name to the Macedonian people. As Nicolaos Papaconstantinou, a former press counselor at the Greek Embassy in the US, demosntrated: '[w]hy should they [the Macedonians] be so adamant if changing their name would give them a future? They should say, 'What's in a name?'"[892] If Greece continues to suggest unrealistic proposals for Macedonia's name and continues to deny reasonable and fair solutions by mediators and negotiators, the negotiation process will never work for this issue or any future issues that will arise between Macedonia and Greece.

---

[887] *UMD Sends Letter to U.S. Secretary of State Condoleezza Rice Regarding Greece.* http://umdiaspora.org/index.php?option=com_content&task=view&id=305&Itemid=1 . Feb. 14th, 2008.

[888] Kentrotis, Kyriakos, *Echoes from the Past: Greece and the Macedonian Controversy*, in '*Mediterranean Politics*', 97 (1994).

[889] International Crisis Group, *Macedonia's Name: Why the Dispute Matters and How to Resolve It*, i (2001).

[890] Seraphinoff, Michael, *Dimensions of the Greek-Macedonian Name Dispute*, 10 (2008).

[891] Frye, Timothy. *Macedonia and EU Integration: Deputy Prime Minister of Macedonia Vasko Naumovski*, February 2010: 1.

[892] *Macedonia is Denied Recognition.* The Rochester Sentinel, August 15th, 1992: 1.

C. Solutions

Macedonians should not compromise on the name of their nation. The problems that divide Macedonia and Greece will only be broadened if such a day comes. Rather, the Macedonians and Greeks should instead collaborate on ways to improve the rights and freedoms of all people, and the economy and stability of both their nations. Further, the roots of the Macedonian-Greek dispute must be confronted without either nation imposing its own history and beliefs on the other. In this spirit, this part is divided in three short sections. First, I discuss why solving the dispute through discussion is the best possible path. Second, I explore some possible solutions. Finally, I confront the likely alternatives to a disintegration of discussions and negotiations.

1. Why resolving the dispute matters

The Macedonian question has been the cause of every great European war for the last fifty years, and until that is settled there will be no more peace either in the Balkans or out of them.[893]

"Collapse in Macedonia would likely delay achievement of a stable, multiethnic Bosnia; damage prospects for peacefully negotiating Kosovo's final status; jeopardize Serbia's democratic transition, and even put question marks over NATO and EU enlargement."[894] Or as Nimetz has stated: "everyone recognises that stability in the region and cooperation is extremely important and cannot be achieved without this issue being resolved."[895] These two statements sum up the potential damaging risks to Macedonian and Balkan security if the name dispute fails to achieve a settlement.

Because Macedonia is a civic state, it is "an anomaly in a region of emphatically 'ethnic' states, three of which uphold fundamental challenges to the Macedonian identity."[896] As much as the Balkan countries try to create ethnically homogenous states, or at least states dominated by one nationality, former Macedonian President Kiril Gligorov acknowledged that "[o]n the ethnically colorfully mixed Balkans it is impossible to form compact nation states, in which only members of one nation live."[897] Macedonia pursued this atypical Balkan path even with the Balkan choir chanting in the background, "[t]his is the Balkans…if you delete nationalities from the constitution, you will die."[898] Still, Greece denies anything associated with the name 'Macedonia,' unless it is associated with Greece; Serbia denies an autonomous Macedonian Orthodox Church; and Bulgaria denies that a Macedonian language and nation exists.[899] If a solution is not found, the idea

[893] Kaplan, Robert D., *Balkan Ghosts: A Journey Throughout History*, 52 (1993). Quote by John Reed.

[894] Evans, Gareth. *Shades of Bosnia: NATO's Plan for Macedonia is Not Sufficient.* Wall Street Journal. http://www.crisisgroup.org/en/regions/europe/balkans/macedonia/evans-shade-of%20Bosnia-natos-plan-for-macedonia-is-not-sufficient.aspx . Aug. 16th, 2001.

[895] *Greece and Macedonia Set New Direct Talks Over Name Dispute.* http://www.earthtimes.org/articles/news/153553.html . Dec. 5th, 2007.

[896] International Crisis Group, *Macedonia's Name: Why the Dispute Matters and How to Resolve It*, i (2001).

[897] Wieland, Carsten, *One Macedonia with Three Faces: Domestic Debates and Nation Concept*, 2.

[898] *Id.*

[899] International Crisis Group, *Macedonia's Name: Why the Dispute Matters and How to Resolve It*, i (2001).

of establishing viable democracies in the Balkans will become a utopian dream. The early 1990s produced a Balkan tragedy, with nations trying to expand their borders by eliminating other ethnicities. Greece's less violent, but more cunning, recent attempts to eradicate Macedonia's fragile existence could reignite these horrors.

For example, Macedonia's government is continuously struggling to maintain legitimacy in the eyes of the international community and its large Albanian minority. If Macedonia continues to hold referendums, it could likely lead to some sort of rejection, which could encourage Albanians to secede from the country, or perhaps to even federalize the government.[900] Martin Schlesinger, an expert at the Woodrow Wilson Institute in Washington, D.C., indicated that a Greek veto of Macedonian accession into NATO could lead to secessionist movements in Macedonia because of Kosovo's recent declaration of independence.[901] Further, it is important to note that "[r]adicals among the Albanians [in Macedonia] have anyway been encouraged by the recent declaration and recognition of Kosovo's independence[,]"[902] and any hint that Macedonia is unsecure and instable could indicate that the moment is opportune to achieve secessionist desires.

As described in this paper, the Balkan Peninsula has experienced several wars since the 1800s, many of them revolving around the Macedonian Question. Thus, when Macedonians and the media see "a video clip showing Greek soldiers in training chanting anti-Macedonian songs,"[903] tensions and fears escalate. Not only does this provoke nationalistic rhetoric from the Macedonians, it instills fear in tiny Macedonia, as wars have torn apart its nation and people. Macedonians continually refer to their Albanian, Bulgarian, Serbian and Greek neighbors as the 'four wolves,'[904] because history has shown their ruthlessness and cunningness in ganging up on her, whether working together, independently or simultaneously, to tear apart the Macedonian people, nation and land. Macedonia cannot ignore such actions, no matter how isolated and infrequent, and still be expected to believe that Greece is negotiating with good faith.

This dispute is between a powerful nation and a tiny nation; it is the smaller Macedonians who should be truly concerned.[905] Although it is difficult enough to deal with one powerful neighbor, Macedonia has to deal with two other powerful neighbors and a restless minority. As recently as in 1990, statements by her other neighbors made Macedonia very weary – the main Serbian opposition party leader, Vuk Draskovic, called for the division of Macedonia by Serbia and Bulgaria; and the Bulgarian and Greek Prime Ministers jointly stated that the Macedonian nation does not exist.[906] A professor at an Albanian-established university in Tetovo, Macedonia even stated that "[t]he Macedonians are a small people who are afraid of being destroyed […] [t]hey have an inferiority complex," and he then called for a separation of ethnic Albanians from Macedonia.[907]

---

[900] Vankin, Sam. *The Republic of North Macedonia and Palestine: Obama Loses Patience With Bush Allies.* June 3, 2009.

[901] Seraphinoff, Michael, *Dimensions of the Greek-Macedonian Name Dispute*, 14 (2008).

[902] *To Name or Not to Name? Greek Nationalism Ltd.*, 7.

[903] *Macedonia protests to Greece over anti-Macedonian video clips.* http://english.people.com.cn/200703/16/eng20070316_358081.html March 16, 2007

[904] Wieland, Carsten, *One Macedonia with Three Faces: Domestic Debates and Nation Concept,* 1.

[905] Vangeli, Anastas, *Antiquity Musing: Reflections on the Greco-Macedonian Symbolic Contest over the Narratives of the Ancient Past*, 20 (2009).

[906] Poulton, Hugh, *The Balkans: Minorities and States in Conflict*, 53-54 (1994).

[907] Chiclet, Christophe, *Macedonia Risks Falling Apart.* http://mondediplo.com/1999/01/13maced

All of this is preached and reiterated, even though history has demonstrated that "[d]enying the existence of Macedonians and their country ... did not help solve the Macedonian problem and did not contribute to Balkan stability in the past, and it will not do so in the future."[908] According to Macedonia's Prime Minister Gruevski, "Macedonia wants a name solution to be found... [because] this is the second biggest problem we are facing."[909] Macedonia does not want to have a problem with her southern neighbor.[910] It does not want a problem with anyone; it has enough problems as a small and economically weak country. Further, "Bulgaria, Serbia, Greece and the Kosovar Albanians, among others, all maintain an active interest in the fate of the fragile Macedonian state. A full-scale war over Macedonia's borders is very unlikely to be confined to Macedonians."[911] Foreign Minister Antonio Milososki reminded Greece that "[t]he name of the Republic of Macedonia is a factor for its stability, and our stability is in Greece's interest."[912]

As mentioned, any delay in finding a solution will affect ethnic relations between Macedonians and Albanians in Macedonia. The large Albanian minority population in Macedonia is less attached to the name issue than ethnic Macedonians;[913] therefore, they could easily cause unrest because they believe this issue is delaying Macedonia's EU and NATO integration. Given the current escalating conflicts with the Albanian minority in Macedonia, allowing Macedonia to use its constitutional name would be in the best interests of promoting peace and good relations in the Balkan region, which is a reason why the UN imposed the name the 'former Yugoslav Republic of Macedonia' in the first place.[914]

The Albanian minority is becoming uneasy with the government's policy of estranging itself from US support and EU support.[915] Thus, the Albanian issue in Macedonia and the affects of ill-compromise with Greece on this Albanian issue cannot be ignored. There has already been past ethnic conflict between Macedonians and Albanians that resulted in much bloodshed. The West either honestly made a mistake, or purposely lied, when they suggested that giving more rights to the Albanians would "remove the root causes of the [2001] war."[916] The root cause is the desire for a Greater Albania:

Even some of the political parties that have represented them [the ethnic Albanians] in

---

[908] *To Name or Not to Name? Greek Nationalism Ltd.*, 7.

[909] *PM Gruevski: I wish a name solution with Greece to be found*   January 19, 2011
http://www.focus-fen.net/index.php?id=n239881

[910] *Macedonia's Gruevski Backs double formula in name dispute*, July 22, 2009
http://www.setimes.com/cocoon/setimes/xhtml/en_GB/newsbriefs/setimes/newsbriefs/2009/07/22/nb-01

[911] Karon, Tony. *Macedonia Contemplates a War of Attrition.*
http://www.time.com/time/world/article/0,8599,103224,00.html Mar. 20th, 2001.

[912] *Macedonia Foreign Minister Rebuffs Greek Threats.*
http://www.balkaninsight.com/en/article/macedonia-foreign-minister-rebuffs-greek-threats . Oct. 15th, 2007.

[913] Vankin, Sam. *The Republic of North Macedonia and Palestine: Obama Loses Patience With Bush Allies.* June 3, 2009.

[914] International Crisis Group, *Macedonia's Name: Why the Dispute Matters and How to Resolve It*, 17 (2001).

[915] *Assessing the Security Implications of Balkan Integration.* 12 (2009).

[916] Fisher, Ian. *Macedonia Peace Signed, but Soon After, Artillery Booms.*
http://select.nytimes.com/gst/abstract.html?res=F60E14F6355B0C778DDDA10894D9404482 . Aug. 13, 2001.

Skopje, however, have lately been calling for the creation of a separate Albanian political entity within a Macedonian federation — an option the government rejects as the first step towards annexing part of Macedonia into a "Greater Albania" along with Kosovo.[917]

The Albanians believed that they could move toward a path of a Greater Albania by fighting to carve off Kosovo, and the "ethnic Albanian guerrilla group that [drew] inspiration and weapons from Kosovo"[918] decided to follow the same path in Macedonia in 2001.

Again, for Albanians, the name of Macedonia is ranked much lower than NATO and EU aspirations.[919] Sacrificing European accession for a name can cause internal security; Albanians could again petition for greater autonomy.[920] The Ohrid Framework still remains fragile, and so is the region, especially neighboring Kosovo.[921] Greece's stance on Macedonia has increased nationalism in Macedonia, which may lead the Albanian minority to "promote its privileges by imposing greater administrative autonomy for the Albanian-dominated areas of Macedonia."[922] This could lead to a Bosnian-styled country, with federalization along ethnic lines.[923] However, this would not be an easy segregation like in Bosnia, where ethnic communities are practically homogeneous.[924] Nearly half of Macedonia's Albanians are minorities in villages, towns and cities,[925] and it is not hard to imagine another Macedonian conflict resembling the one it experienced 2001. Before Greece's veto, Macedonia feared that secession by Serbs in Kosovo could lead to the same in Macedonia; now, the threat of secession of Albanians in Macedonia could lead to the secession of Albanians in southern Serbia and Serbs in Kosovo,[926] potentially even leading to more secessionist movements in Serbia and Bosnia. The effect of this could then lead to Macedonian secessionist movements in Albania, where it estimated that there could be over 100,000 Macedonians,[927] and in Bulgaria and Greece, where we have already seen that large Macedonian populations exist.

Certainly, Macedonia's recognition of Kosovo as an independent country helped to temporarily appease the local Albanians.[928] But that decision does not come without consequences. It did not appease the neighboring Serbs, who are far bigger and stronger than Macedonia and the Albanians. Further, ethnic tensions with Albanians still manifest themselves in the form of violence, as an ethnic brawl in Skopje over the creation of a religious museum demonstrated. The Albanians in Macedonia are becoming impatient.[929]

---

[917] Karon, Tony. *Macedonia Contemplates a War of Attrition.* http://www.time.com/time/world/article/0,8599,103224,00.html Mar. 20th, 2001.

[918] *A Fragile Peace for Macedonia.* http://select.nytimes.com/gst/abstract.html?res=F30B12F7355B0C778DDDA10894D9404482 . Aug. 14th, 2001.

[919] *Assessing the Security Implications of Balkan Integration.* 18 (2009).

[920] *Id.*

[921] International Crisis Group, *Macedonia's Name: Breaking the Deadlock,* 13 (2009).

[922] Matovski, Aleksandar. *Macedonia After Bucharest: Avoiding Another European Failure in the Balkans,* 4 (2008).

[923] *Id.*

[924] *Id.*

[925] *Id.*

[926] *Id.* at 5.

[927] Poulton, Hugh, *The Balkans: Minorities and States in Conflict,* 201 (1994).

[928] International Crisis Group, *Macedonia's Name: Breaking the Deadlock,* 5 (2009)..

[929] *Id.*

When will this impatience turn into another armed conflict?

There is also the potential for a political and armed revolution in Aegean Macedonia. Many Macedonians in Aegean Macedonia live in fear due to constant police surveillance.[930] In 2001, Albanian terrorists waged war on Macedonia, justifying it as a fight "to use their language […] denied [to] them" by the Macedonians.[931] As evidenced by UN committees and human rights committees, Macedonians face an even more severe situation in Greece, as well as in Albania and Bulgaria. If the Albanians were rewarded with greater rights through armed conflict, what is to discourage Macedonians from doing the same in surrounding countries when they face more deplorable conditions than the Albanians did in Macedonia? For centuries Macedonians have been fighting and struggling for equal rights. They have feared the consequences of displaying their identity; and this fear may evolve into unchecked anger and hatred. As expressed by Macedonians living in Albania:

> Albanian government officials, secret service agents, and police have tried to prevent the classes from taking place and have issued death threats against the Macedonian [language] teachers[.] […] "We feel like third class citizens. We feel degraded; how can it be that we live in a country in the 21st century, with a police force that bans the learning of one's mother tongue?", asked an angry Edmond Osmani, President of the Golo Brdo local committee of the Macedonian Alliance for European Integration.[932]

In the Balkans, how long can a deprived and discriminated against community go without some sort of violent rebellion? History has taught us not that long.

While internal and regional peace is in jeopardy, so is the economic prosperity of both Macedonia and Greece. Greece is Macedonia's second largest foreign investor.[933] Between 1994 and 2004, Greek exports to Macedonia increased over ten-fold, while Macedonian exports to Greece exploded almost twenty-fold.[934] "Greek private businesses gobbled up everything Macedonian - tobacco companies, catering cum hotel groups, mining complexes, travel agencies - at bargain basement prices[.]"[935] Macedonia's oil refinery in 1999 was sold to a Greek company, and many Macedonian banks are mostly or partly controlled by Greek banks.[936]A cut in ties could be economically devastating to both countries because Greece is one of Macedonia's largest investors,[937] and Greece's currently failing economy needs all the support it can get. For example, Greece exports

---

[930] Human Rights Watch, *Denying Ethnic Identity: The Macedonians in Greece*, 55 (1994).

[931] McNeil, Jr., Donald G., *NATO is Sending British Troops to Macedonia for Disarmament*.
http://select.nytimes.com/gst/abstract.html?res=F60911FB3F5A0C758DDDA10894D9404482 . August 15th, 2001.

[932] *Macedonians in Albania Demand End to Discrimination*.
http://www.mhrmi.org/news/2010/december10_e.asp . Dec. 10th, 2002.

[933] Vankin, Sam. *The Republic of North Macedonia and Palestine: Obama Loses Patience With Bush Allies*. June 3, 2009.

[934] Axt, Heinz-Jurgen et. al., *The Greek Macedonian Name Dispute -- Reconciliation through Europeanization?*, 23 (2006).

[935] Vankin, Sam. *Greeks Bearing Gifts – Greek Investments in the Balkans*.
http://www.globalpolitician.com/print.asp?id=1135

[936] *Id*.

[937] Axt, Heinz-Jurgen et. al., *The Greek Macedonian Name Dispute -- Reconciliation through Europeanization?*, 23 (2006).

more to Macedonia than it does either to France or Canada.[938]

An economic depression occurred in Macedonia after the Greek veto on Macedonia's accession into NATO, when not only did the Macedonian stock market index fall by over 8%, all businesses in Macedonia were negatively affected, including Greek-based companies.[939] It is projected that this veto is having the effect of redirecting foreign investments away from Macedonia and decreasing the credit rating of Macedonia.[940] Macedonians are being forced to choose between their identity and a bright economic future. A 'solution' that ignores one of these aspects is no solution at all.

Macedonia further risks becoming isolated from a European path and the international community if a fair solution is not found. First, the Macedonian electorate will begin to detest European integration.[941] As the late President Boris Trajkovski stated in an interview, "[o]ur citizens will lose their confidence or trust in the values and principles of the international community…if our personal identity is denied."[942] As also evidenced by the 2009 ICG report, Macedonians' faith in international goodwill was already undermined when NATO and EU allowed Greece to violate the interim accord by blocking Macedonia's integration in international organizations.[943] Second, politicians will use such a rejection by NATO and the EU to promote nationalistic interests[944] other than those of getting accession into NATO or the EU. Because Greece is blocking Macedonia's accession into these organizations, it is becoming increasingly politically costlier for Skopje to justify time and expense in pursuing NATO accession and participating in NATO missions in Kosovo, Bosnia, and Iraq.[945] "[T]elling Macedonia that it should find a solution to the 'name dispute' means ... telling Macedonians to accept changes in its name and identity and there is a danger that the public opinion will turn against the EU and the NATO."[946] This danger is not that the EU and NATO will feel threatened by Macedonia – they will not. However, there are numerous economic and political benefits for these two international institutions if Macedonia is incorporated into them. A critical step in promoting Balkan and European strategic interests in the Balkans is to integrate the Balkan countries into NATO.[947] A European Parliament member further stated that "EU membership is not only beneficial for Macedonia and the region, but for EU as well, because Europe cannot be united without Western Balkan nations."[948] By vetoing Macedonia's NATO bid, Greece is promoting interests opposite to these interests,

---

[938] Id.

[939] Taleski, Dane, *Macedonia After the Greek Veto for Membership in NATO: Analysis of the Effects and the Situation*, 5 (2008).

[940] Id.

[941] Petrovic, Jelena and Marko Savkovic. *No Carrot? Why Comply?*, 8.

[942] Vankin, Sam. *Man of Vision: Interview with the President of the Republic of Macedonia Mr. Boris Trajkovski*.

[943] International Crisis Group, *Macedonia's Name: Breaking the Deadlock*, 1 (2009).

[944] Petrovic, Jelena and Marko Savkovic. *No Carrot? Why Comply?*, 8.

[945] McNamara, Sally. *It is Past Time for Macedonia to Join NATO*. January 2010: 1.

[946] Slaveski, Stojan. *Macedonian Strategic Culture and Institutional Choice: Integration or Isolation?* 50 (2009).

[947] Taleski, Dane, *Macedonia After the Greek Veto for Membership in NATO: Analysis of the Effects and the Situation*, 5 (2008).

[948] *Kukan-Naumovski: Macedonia Belongs to the European Family*, http://www.mia.com.mk/default.aspx?vId=81361516&lId=2 . February 21, 201.

and this impedes the likeliness of a stable Balkan region.[949]

Furthermore, what kind of examples do Greece's actions set for other countries that are struggling to achieve viable democracies or for nations confronted with ethnic challenges? "If a country (Macedonia) has reached the satisfactory level in compliance and its results … and still, has not received the reward – it is to be expected the significant decrease of dedication to compliance among its population and political elite."[950] Through denying Macedonian acceptance into NATO and the EU, the West is basically telling small countries everywhere that rules and compliance do not matter as much as politics and special interests. Hence, when considering Europeanizing future countries and regions through NATO and EU enlargement, members now have precedent, thanks to a Greek veto on Macedonia's accession due to Macedonia's name, to veto stabilization of any region, for any reason.[951] As Dane Talevski suggests, this is "[r]e-Balkanization instead of Europeanization."[952]

However, the reasons for finding a solution are not only to avoid negative consequences, but to create positives. As Nimetz stated, "[t]his is one that cries out for a solution because the positives of solving it are so great."[953] Particularly, Nimetz mentioned how the EU and NATO processes would be enhanced.[954] Thus, there are also advantages for Greece to finding a solution. By not compromising, "Greece is depriving itself of substantial potential revenue and is going against its own interests."[955] For example, Greece could be more effective politically and economically in the Mediterranean region if it spends less time "managing its northern neighbor."[956] The economic advantages would extend beyond the 834 million US dollars Greece and Macedonia had in the trade exchange in 2007, and the over 50 million Euros that Macedonian tourists invest in the Greek economy each year.[957]

Yet, even though a resolution "could help restore a sense of security and contribute to normalization in the southern Balkans,"[958] this depends on the result. For example, if Greece recognizes the Macedonian identity, then it might have to recognize that a Macedonian minority exists within its borders. If Greece does not recognize a Macedonian minority, can the international community honestly suggest that normalization has reached the southern Balkans? A US Department of State's Country Report in 1993 stated that Macedonians who engage in public dissent regarding Macedonian and minority issues

---

[949] Taleski, Dane, *Macedonia After the Greek Veto for Membership in NATO: Analysis of the Effects and the Situation*, 4 (2008).
[950] Petrovic, Jelena and Marko Savkovic. *No Carrot? Why Comply?*, 8.
[951] Taleski, Dane, *Macedonia After the Greek Veto for Membership in NATO: Analysis of the Effects and the Situation*, 5 (2008).
[952] *Id.*
[953] *Greece, Macedonia to Meet Over Name Dispute.* http://bdnews24.com/details.php?id=84130&cid=4 . Dec. 5th, 2007.
[954] *Id.*
[955] Kosanic, Zoran, *Obstacle's to FYROM's Membership of NATO: A Tougher Agenda Than Expected.* 4 (2009).
[956] Kosanic, Zoran, Obstacle's to FYROM's Membership of NATO: A Tougher Agenda Than Expected. Research Division -- NATO Defense College, No. 44. February, 2009. Pg. 4.
[957] Taleski, Dane, *Macedonia After the Greek Veto for Membership in NATO: Analysis of the Effects and the Situation*, 5 (2008).
[958] http://news.bbc.co.uk/2/hi/europe/1737425.stm .

would have a difficult time pursuing an academic career in Greece.[959] There is no fair treatment in schools, as evidenced by the following anecdote:

> "A history teacher told a sophomore class that Macedonians were 'gypsies, with no culture.' One boy asked why the teacher had said that; 'aren't they human beings like us?' The student was sent to the superintendent's office; later his parents were called in and warned to prevent the child from making such remarks."[960]

Fair treatment at the borders does not exist, where ethnic Macedonians are still harassed and subjected to "aggressive interrogations."[961] There is no fair treatment of Macedonians in Greece with respect to cultural displays, such as "performing songs in the Macedonian language and traditional dances."[962] A solution is necessary, but a solution to the name dispute will only bring normalization if the Macedonian minority issue is addressed.

The fear was, and still is, that Macedonia could become a 'Palestine in the Balkans'[963] if a just and meaningful solution is not found. Macedonia does not want this, Europe does not want this, and the world cannot accept this result. The dispute needs to be resolved soon – but how?

2. Possible paths to a solution?

Macedonian culture belongs to the entire world -- it is something that should unite all countries and civilizations that have been built on this heritage.[964]

Certainly, a solution can and has to be found. Not even two years into the name dispute, Europe was "sick and tired of this problem."[965] Twenty years later, the international community is still puzzled and struggling to devise ways to move forward. The dragged-out process has not left the world without hope of a solution, but it has instilled a major doubt and confusion as to what is actually necessary to settle the dispute.

The negotiation process has at times employed the practice of caucusing, leaving Nimetz to shuffle from the Greeks to the Macedonians with new name solutions. Speaking on behalf of a proposed name solution, the Macedonian President at the time, Branko Crvenkovski, "said he did not know whether the latest proposal indeed came from Nimetz" or from Greece.[966] He thought it also could have been "a possible way for Greece to

---

[959] Human Rights Watch, *Denying Ethnic Identity: The Macedonians in Greece*, 56 (1994).

[960] Human Rights Watch, *Denying Ethnic Identity: The Macedonians in Greece*, 57 (1994).

[961] Gay McDougall Mission to Greece, *Promotion and Protection of All Human Rights, Civil, Political, Economic, Social and Cultural Rights, Including the Right to Development*, 14 (2009).

[962] *Id.*

[963] Warne, Leslie, *We Exist, Say Illawarra Macedonians*, http://www.greenleft.org.au/node/2031 Mar. 11th, 1992.

[964] Frye, Timothy. *Macedonia and EU Integration: Deputy Prime Minister of Macedonia Vasko Naumovski*. February 2010: 2.

[965] Lambert, Sarah. *Greek Refusal to Recognise Macedonia Comes Under Fire.* http://www.independent.co.uk/news/world/europe/greek-refusal-to-recognise-macedonia-comes-under-fire-1479801.html . Jan. 21st, 1993.

[966] *Macedonia: New Developments in Name Row With Greece.* www.rferl.org/content/article/1058423.html . Apr. 13th, 2005.

approach us."[967] Perhaps certain Greek officials are tired of their current stance on the Macedonian name and identity and do not want to officially appear that they are the ones suggesting meaningful steps to a compromise on the name. Caucusing allows name solutions to be suggested with the Greek people attributing blame to the international community and not their own elected politicians. Although this caucusing could backfire and the Greeks could demand an exit from talks, it could also allow Greek officials to escape from past nationalistic and unreasonable stances without betraying Greek pride.

Plenty of solutions have been proffered in the past by other neutral parties. For example, the ESI suggested that Macedonia should amend its constitution to state that it will change its name once Macedonia joins the EU.[968] Of course, such a solution negates the identity problem and self-determination problem, and assumes that the EU is more important than a name or identity, and promotes an outside political and financial view that EU aspiration should be more important than a name or identity. The Macedonians cannot accept this. Still, novel attempts to find solutions should not be discarded, as coming to a solution requires creative input and collaboration. It never hurts to suggest untenable ideas as long as they are made with a good-faith intention to solve the rift and prevent future violence.

For its creative input, the ICG stated that a solution should entail, in part, each country avoiding the use of references in their educational curricula that offend the other nation's sensitivities.[969] The ICG does not seem to account for the difficulty in actually making this happen. Any suggestion in the Republic of Macedonia's educational system that ethnic Macedonians are related to ancient Macedonians will offend the Greek nation's sensitivities. It brings up the question of whether one nation should be cautious about how it approaches its ethnic identity in order not to offend another nation's attachment to history. Still, such a proposed solution could be the foundation of serious collaboration between Greece and Macedonia on the issue of ancient and modern history. Such a joint commission of historians could be similar to what France and Germany did after World War II.[970] Macedonian Foreign Minister Milososki advocated this in a letter to his Greek counterpart. "I believe that one of the possible steps for building a confidence between the two countries and nations is a joint review of the historic events," wrote Milososki.[971]

However, any proposed solution by any party, neutral or not, will only be successful if it incorporates all issues. First, Macedonia and Macedonians cannot compromise on issues of identity, such as their language, religion and constitutional use of their name. Second, Greece has to acknowledge the internationally established problems it has created with regards to its Macedonian minority, and then seek reforms and pathways to improving the rights and conditions of these Macedonians.

Ancient Macedonia comprises only one part of the Greek identity, whereas for the

---

[967] *Macedonia: New Developments in Name Row With Greece.* www.rferl.org/content/article/1058423.html . Apr. 13th, 2005.
[968] *Macedonia name dispute inspires exotic idea.*
http://www.euractiv.com/en/enlargement/macedonia-name-dispute-inspires-exotic-idea-news-496249 July 12, 2010.
[969] International Crisis Group, *Macedonia's Name: Breaking the Deadlock*, 2 (2009).
[970] *Id.* at 13.
[971] *FM Milososki Sends Letter to Greek Counterpart, Suggests Establishing of Good-Neighborly Relations.* http://www.mia.com.mk/default.aspx?vId=63024083&lId=2 .

Macedonian identity, Macedonia constitutes the entire Macedonian identity.[972] It is true that both Slavic ancestry and ancient Macedonian glory contribute to the Macedonian identity, but these two do not necessarily conflict with one another.[973] In fending off adversarial interests against her by her neighbors, Macedonia utilizes a Slavic connection to ward off Greek and Albanian interests, while it uses an ancient Macedonian connection to ward off Serbian and Bulgarian influence.[974] Nonetheless, Greece wants Macedonia to "repudiate the Communist concept of 'Macedonism'"[975] and thus force the Macedonians to redefine their ethnicity. Any solution to the dispute must not allow for this, as it jeopardizes internationally established laws and principles of self-determination.

Already, the Ohrid Framework Agreement dilutes the sentiment that Macedonians have a homeland by giving substantially more rights to ethnic minorities[976] that other Balkan nations do not give to their minorities. For example, Macedonia is the only civic state in the Balkans; the other countries basically state they are nations with one dominant ethnic people. While Macedonia should not revert back to such a governing mentality, it cannot be expected to compromise on issues of identity, especially when its surrounding nations are doing less to even accommodate ethnic and minority rights into their governing structures, and especially when Macedonia is the most threatened nation by its neighbors on this matter.

Greek negotiators insist that they are ready to find an acceptable name, but they still are adamantly "opposed to the population and language of FYROM being described as 'Macedonians.'"[977] This further solidifies the fears Macedonians have that their identity will be changed if their country's name is changed to north-, new-, or upper-Macedonia.[978] In respect to international law and the Interim Accord, Macedonia's constitutionally chosen name and its national identity are not something that should be compromised for under the guise of a 'name dispute'.[979] If this continues to be a problem for Macedonia, then "Macedonia must stop the UN talks and ask for a new resolution which would also affirm the use of the constitutional name of Macedonia within the UN system."[980] This is not a desirable path because it undermines the international process and ditches the negotiation process. However, Macedonia cannot be asked to negotiate matters that Greece or any other nation would not be expected to negotiate on if they were in Macedonia's position.

Further, as mentioned, any solution should incorporate the ethnic Macedonian rights in Greece. When Greece acknowledges that a Macedonian minority exists, Macedonians will probably believe that their identity is in less jeopardy. A 1994 Human Rights Watch Report in Greece concluded the following with regard to Macedonians in

---

[972] International Crisis Group, *Macedonia's Name: Breaking the Deadlock*, 3 (2009).

[973] Vangeli, Anastas, *Antiquity Musing: Reflections on the Greco-Macedonian Symbolic Contest over the Narratives of the Ancient Past*, 58 (2009).

[974] *Id.*

[975] Kentrotis, Kyriakos. *Echoes from the Past: Greece and the Macedonian Controversy*, in '*Mediterranean Politics*', 98 (1994).

[976] International Crisis Group, *Macedonia's Name: Breaking the Deadlock*, 1 (2009).

[977] Kosanic, Zoran, *Obstacle's to FYROM's Membership of NATO: A Tougher Agenda Than Expected. February, 2009. Pg. 3.*

[978] Seraphinoff, Michael, *Dimensions of the Greek-Macedonian Name Dispute*, 2 (2008).

[979] Taleski, Dane. *Macedonia After the Greek Veto for Membership in NATO: Analysis of the Effects and the Situation*, April, 2008: 6.

[980] *To Name or Not to Name? Greek Nationalism Ltd.*, 7.

Greece: an ethnic Macedonian minority with its own language and culture exists in Greece; the Greek government has violated international human rights laws by denying that a Macedonian group exists; freedom of expression is restricted for ethnic Macedonians; the Greek government discriminates against Macedonians in violation of international laws and agreements to which it is a party; ethnic Macedonian political refugees from the Greek Civil War are denied right to regain citizenship, resettle, or visit northern Greece, while ethnic Greeks are granted such rights; the teaching of the Macedonian language is not permitted; and government forces harass Macedonian rights activists.[981] Some of the things that Macedonians need from the Greek government in Aegean Macedonia is freedom of movement across borders to visit family members; a change in the Greek law so that all political refugees can return; a right to education in the Macedonian language; freedom of association for Macedonians; land for landless peasants; and cross frontier cooperation,[982] and equality before the law and state.[983]

Greece has to redefine its interpretation of what a minority is, because it is currently too restrictive.[984] It cannot simply suggest that the idea of ethnic minority communities existing within its borders is politically motivated.[985] For example, the word 'minority' cannot be implied to mean 'foreign,' as doing so renders these minorities as "conspirators against the interest of the Greek state."[986] If the Greek government does not like the actions or statements of a particular ethnic group or person, it currently can simply utilize this definition to brand these people as criminals. In essence, Greece has used language manipulation to maintain itself as nation with a political and social hierarchy based on ethnic affiliation.

Any change in how Greece approaches the minority issue should require that Greece respects and implements the European Convention on Human Rights, which states in part that "the enjoyment of the rights and freedoms ... shall be secured without discrimination on any ground such as sex, race, color, language, religion, political or other opinion, national or social origin, association with a national minority[.]"[987] Greece should also respect the Universal Declaration on Human Rights, which states that "[a]ll are equal before the law and are entitled without any discrimination to equal protection of the law."[988] Greek policies that violate these international laws include "admitting 'Greek Greeks' who fought against the government during the civil war, but not ethnic Macedonians or their descendants."[989] If Greece reverses these discriminatory policies as part of a solution with regards to the name dispute, Macedonia and Greece will be attacking some of the roots of the recent conflict between Greece and Macedonia – which is the only way to achieve a lasting peace.

So how can Greece go about "retreat[ing] from the dispute over whether there is a Macedonian minority" and begin "protecting the rights to self-determination, freedom of

---

[981] Human Rights Watch, *Denying Ethnic Identity: The Macedonians in Greece*, 2-3 (1994).
[982] *Id*. at 49.
[983] *Id*. at 50.
[984] Gay McDougall Mission to Greece, *Promotion and Protection of All Human Rights, Civil, Political, Economic, Social and Cultural Rights, Including the Right to Development*, 21 (2009).
[985] *Id*.
[986] *Id*. at 22.
[987] Human Rights Watch, *Denying Ethnic Identity: The Macedonians in Greece*, 27 (1994).
[988] Human Rights Watch, *Denying Ethnic Identity: The Macedonians in Greece*, 27 (1994).
[989] *Id*. at 29.

expressions, and freedom of association[?]"[990] First, Greece has to recognize the Macedonian ethnicity. If Greece does not recognize the Macedonian ethnicity, recognition of a Macedonian minority is impossible. Second, Greece has to recognize the ethnic Macedonian minority within its borders. Greece is "a Western country and [the] self-proclaimed 'birthplace of democracy[.]'"[991] It is absurd to believe that a European nation could proclaim that it is ethnically pure in the 21st century. Third, Greece has to stop intimidating this Macedonian minority. When ethnic Macedonians in Greece protested the Greek Army's heavy military maneuvers near their village, the Greek army "'broke arms and legs, violently dragged women and children from the street' and arrested eight people."[992] Greece instead needs to use its police forces to protect the Macedonian minority. In 2009, when ethnic Macedonians in Greece were presenting Greece's first Macedonian-Greek dictionary, Greek neo-Nazis publicly announced they would interrupt such event.[993] The police ignored this threat, and neo-Nazis aggressively provoked ethnic Macedonians, interrupting their presentation.[994] Fortunately, no one was hurt. However, if such intimidation is allowed to continue without state protection, the recognition of a Macedonian minority will be meaningless and potentially dangerous to the lives of Macedonians living in Greece.

Thus, Macedonians cannot cave into Greece's unfair demands. Instead, Macedonia should reiterate its demands. For example, Macedonia could request that Greece guarantees it does not have territorial aspirations for the Republic of Macedonia,[995] such as by requiring Greece to amend its constitution to state so. Or, even though the ICG report suggests that Macedonia should rename its Skopje airport back to its original name,[996] Macedonia should consider this only if Greece renames its Thesaloniki airport back to its original name. Macedonia could even insist that the UN examine the illegality of the conditions set upon it to join UN, as the right of a country to choose its own name is derived from self-determination.[997] By setting certain conditions to join, the UN violated its own charter, particularly Article 2, which states that the UN shall not interfere in matters of domestic jurisdiction and further discusses the principles of sovereignty.[998] Furthermore, the UN's labeling of Macedonia as 'the former Yugoslav Republic of Macedonia' instead of as her constitutional name violates the Vienna Convention, which holds that no discrimination shall exist between states.[999] With this dispute not only are Macedonians facing a threat to their existence and interests, but they are championing the rights and

---

[990] Gay McDougall Mission to Greece, *Promotion and Protection of All Human Rights, Civil, Political, Economic, Social and Cultural Rights, Including the Right to Development*, 24 (2009).

[991] Quote by Bill Nicholov. *Canadian Citizen Denied Entry into Greece Because of Macedonian Ethnicity.* http://www.mhrmi.org/news/2007/october30b_e.asp . Oct. 30th, 2007.

[992] *Greece Steps Up Blatant Attacks on Human Rights Activists and Macedonian Minority.* http://www.mhrmi.org/news/2008/october18_e.asp . October 18th, 2008.

[993] *Greek Neo-Nazis Disrupt Presentation of the First Greek-Macedonian Dictionary in Athens.* June 3, 2009. Macedonian Human Rights Movement International.

[994] *Id.*

[995] Taleski, Dane. *Macedonia After the Greek Veto for Membership in NATO: Analysis of the Effects and the Situation,,* April, 2008: 6.

[996] International Crisis Group, *Macedonia's Name: Breaking the Deadlock*, 2 (2009).

[997] Bajalski, Borko, *Legal Aspects of Macedonia and Greece Name Dispute in Relation to UN Charter, the Interim Accord, and Macedonia's Integration to NATO/EU*, 9 (2009).

[998] *Id.*

[999] *Id.* at10.

freedoms that are fundamental to creating a peaceful and stable world.

Macedonia and Greece have a shared duty to act constructively.[1000] Greece and Macedonia should also share a common commitment to peace, stability, and sustainable development.[1001] There have been plenty of signs outside the scope of the negotiation process which have led to some collaborative efforts between Greece and Macedonia. In a sense, Macedonia has had little choice, as Greece is a major factor in its economy – it is almost as if Greece has had a monopoly over Macedonia. But collaboration has happened. During the 1999 Kosovo War and the 2001 Macedonian Albanian insurgency, Greece helped Macedonia, giving humanitarian assistance and financial support.[1002] During this time period, the two countries signed an Agreement on Military Co-operation,[1003] and the Greek Foreign Minister visited Macedonia several times, expressing Greece's support for Macedonia.[1004] Scholarships allow Macedonian cadets to attend military academies in Greece;[1005] the Greek Ministry of Defense also gives financial assistance for housing renovation and minor reconstruction projects in Macedonia;[1006] the two countries signed a Protocol on Police Co-operation;[1007] Greece has provided several million dollars in creating a wastewater facility in Strumica, Macedonia;[1008] and along with Albania, Greece and Macedonia have been collaborating on creating an International Park in Lake Prespa.[1009] There are strengths to collaboration, and Macedonia and Greece must confront this dispute with this positive spirit.

If not, the only thing that may be able to ensure a viable solution is sustained international pressure on Greece. The last time Greece was in the position of "a basket case constantly in need of EC economic aid,"[1010] the European Community was reluctant to strongly condemn Greece. But a change in current Greek attitude toward name dispute might be possible because of its current economic problems.[1011] These realities give NATO and EU significant leverage over Greece[1012] that they should not be unwilling to utilize if Greece continues advocating positions that simply create more obstacles. International financial organizations and Western countries have given much financial support to Greece through this current difficult period for Greece, and "it is time for Greece to reciprocate that friendship…"[1013] It is an opportune time for the West to pressure Greece, highlight Macedonia's involvement in and contribution to the Iraq and

---

[1000] *Assessing the Security Implications of Balkan Integration.* 12 (2009)..

[1001] Kondonis, Haralambos. *Bilateral Relations Between Greece and the Former Yugoslav Republic of Macedonia*, 86.

[1002] *Id.* at 59.

[1003] *Id.* at 61.

[1004] *Id.* at 60.

[1005] *Id.* at 62.

[1006] *Id.*

[1007] *Id.* at 64.

[1008] *Id.* at 70.

[1009] *Id.* at 69.

[1010] Gelb, Leslie H., *Foreign Affairs; 'Macedonia' for Greece*, http://select.nytimes.com/gst/abstract.html?res=F10613F93C5F0C718DDDAF0894DA494D81 Jun. 12th, 1992.

[1011] *Assessing the Security Implications of Balkan Integration.* 21 (2009).

[1012] *Assessing the Security Implications of Balkan Integration.* 21 (2009).

[1013] McNamara, Sally and Morgan L. Roach, *The Obama Administration Must Push for Macedonia's Accession to NATO at the Lisbon Summit*, The Heritage Foundation. Web Memo No. 3037, 1 (2010).

Afghanistan mission,[1014] and let Macedonia into NATO. This would not be akin to forcing Greece to sacrifice its identity for economic gain; it would simply be reminding Greece that it faces consequences for not being a just or positive force in the Balkans.

However, Macedonian PM Gruevski notes that "the current financial crisis in Greece has caused EU countries to be more careful towards Greece, because the country's economic issues also create political repercussions."[1015] This is demonstrated by some Greek officials' current attitude. Instead of blaming themselves, some of Greece's government officials are suggesting that Germany has not sufficiently paid Greece back for Nazi occupation during World War II. [1016] This rhetoric allows Greece to refuse responsibility for the problems it has created for itself and its neighbors. A solution may be for the international community to no longer tolerate a Greek attitude that ignores its duties and obligations as a member of the international community. As of right now, Europe has only shown Greece the carrot, not the stick.

Solutions through negotiations and discussions are the most desired solutions. Sometimes, the international community and outside forces should responsibly inject themselves in order to encourage the parties back on the right track, without violating or trespassing on the parties' rights and freedoms. However, as two decades of tense negotiations are starting to demonstrate, the negotiation process does not always work. Thus, when two countries reach this point, what options do they have left?

3. Alternatives to a compromise

There are two visible paths to which failed discussions could lead. First, the status quo could continue for decades, leaving Macedonia and Greece in an ethnically tense atmosphere. Second, there is a chance that the international court systems could confront the dispute and impose a solution. Yet, it is unlikely that any court decision will have anything other than a symbolic impact on the dispute.

Macedonia has some incentive not to negotiate. Already, over 130 nations have recognized Macedonia as the Republic of Macedonia, which is nearly two-thirds of the world's countries. Further, as a 2008 Gallup Poll indicated, Macedonia's neighbors overwhelmingly agree with her on the name issue: 60% of respondents within Macedonia, Albania, Serbia, Montenegro, Kosovo, and Bosnia and Herzegovina stated that even if Greece was against the Republic of Macedonia being called Macedonia, they would support Macedonia being called Macedonia; only just over 10% of respondents would be against Macedonia's decision.[1017] As the Macedonian Foreign Minister stated in 1993, which applies to the sentiment today: "the moment we give up on our name, the question

---

[1014] *Id.* at 2.
[1015] *PM Gruevski: I wish a name solution with Greece to be found* January 19, 2011, http://www.focus-fen.net/index.php?id=n239881
[1016] *Greece Must Reform Politically as Well as Economically.*
http://greatersurbiton.wordpress.com/2010/02/28/greece-must-reform-politically-as-well-as-economically/ .
Feb. 28th, 2010.
[1017] English, Cynthia. *Balkan Nations at Odds with Greece Over Macedonia's Name.*
http://www.gallup.com/poll/105091/balkan-nations-odds-greece-over-macedonias-name.aspx . Mar. 18th, 2008.

will arise: if you're not Macedonians then who are you?"[1018] The peoples of the other Balkan nations recognize this; yet, Greece seems not to accept this as a valid concern. Thus, it is becoming less likely that Macedonia will continue negotiating on its name.

Furthermore, Macedonia believes that Greece has come to a standstill in negotiations. According to Gruevski, the "Greek leadership has been successfully selling the story for almost a year that it is very interested in a swift solution and that progress is being made."[1019] With this attitude by Greece, it is obviously hard for a solution to be reached. Further, Gruevski's words are not simply an attempt to pass off blame, as this paper has established that Greece is no longer willing to concede anything, signifying the end of serious Greek participation in negotiations. As the Greek Foreign Minister stated in 2010, "Greece ha[s] actively proved its desire to contribute to finding a mutually acceptable solution to the issue of the name to be used by FYROM and that it was now up to the neighbouring country to 'cover the corresponding distance' in order to arrive at a mutually acceptable name."[1020] These words and actions make Macedonian officials believe that Greece is only interested in handshakes and photo-ops, and thus are no longer pragmatic about the dispute.[1021] Hence, there is unwillingness by Macedonians to further seriously negotiate if the Greeks are not seriously going to negotiate.

As a matter of fact, in February 2008, a Macedonian government spokesperson stated that a Greek veto of Macedonia's accession into NATO would nullify the 1995 Interim Accord, which would allow Macedonia to revoke it.[1022] A revoking of the Interim Accord might result in Macedonia seriously attempting to be recognized in the UN as the Republic of Macedonia; a reinstatement of Macedonia's original flag; pressure on Greece to recognizing the Macedonian minority in Greece and return properties to ethnic Macedonian political refugees; rename Macedonian places after ancient Macedonians; and develop closer ties with traditional Greek adversaries, such as Turkey.[1023] We have already seen the Macedonians pursue some of these goals since the 2008 veto.

Furthermore, the EU's policy regarding unanimity for accepting a member may change by 2018, and Macedonia could theoretically wait that long for accession.[1024] But Macedonia would still have to negotiate with Greece to enter into NATO.[1025] Yet, Macedonia has patiently withstood two decades of Greek bullying and unfair treatment, while becoming an example for developing nations worldwide with its commitment to democracy and international principles. Holding out on a compromised solution just a little longer may bring more aid and support for Macedonia. As a former UN mediator of the name dispute, Robert O'Neil stated: "Macedonia must not and will not change its name in

[1018] Zahariadis, Nikolaos. *External Interventions and Domestic Ethnic Conflict in Yugoslav Macedonia.* Political Science Quarterly. 118(2). Summer, 2003: 268.
[1019] *PM Gruevski: I wish a name solution with Greece to be found,* January 19, 2011, http://www.focus-fen.net/index.php?id=n239881
[1020] *FM outlines foreign policy to Greek ambassadors* http://www.ana.gr/anaweb/user/showplain?maindoc=5571641&maindocimg=5435499&service=10 Sep, 12, 2010.
[1021] Macedonia says Greece lacks pragmatism over name issue. http://english.people.com.cn/90001/90777/90853/6932410.html, March 27, 2010.
[1022] Seraphinoff, Michael, *Dimensions of the Greek-Macedonian Name Dispute,* 10 (2008).
[1023] *Id.*
[1024] Kosanic, Zoran, *Obstacle's to FYROM's Membership of NATO: A Tougher Agenda Than Expected.* 2009: 7.
[1025] *Id.*

order to appease Greece. If Macedonia succumbs to pressures and changes its name, such events will only give more firepower to Greece until it reaches its final goal - Macedonia to vanish from the map."[1026] Macedonia knows the world supports Macedonia – the only question is for how long can Macedonia survive the storm without jeopardizing all the progress it has made so far?

The second main way the issue may be potentially solved is through the international court system. The two countries are currently in court, and after over two years, the ICJ has heard oral arguments between Macedonia and Greece. "[Macedonia] contends that the Hellenic Republic violated its rights under Article 11 by objecting ... to its application to join NATO... in particular ... because Greece desires 'to resolve the difference between the Parties concerning the constitutional name of the Applicant as an essential precondition'" to join NATO. [1027] Thus, Macedonia insists that Greece "'immediately take[s] all necessary steps to comply with its obligations under Article 11, paragraph 1 [of the Interim Accord]' and ... 'cease[s] and desist[s] from objecting in any way, whether directly or indirectly, to [Macedonia's] membership of [NATO] and/or of any other 'international, multilateral and regional organizations and institutions' of which [Greece] is a member'[.]"[1028]

Greece argues that there is legality to support blocking Macedonia from entering into NATO. Particularly, they point to Article 10 of the NATO Treaty, which states that nations have to be "in a position to further the principles of [the] Treaty" and must "promot[e] conditions of stability."[1029] The Greek Ministry of Foreign Affairs insists that it is the instability caused by the name dispute with Greece that resulted in the veto.[1030] This is because "[t]he Court cannot determine 'the reasons which, in the mind of a Member, may prompt its vote' on admission of another State to membership in an organization; rather, 'the question can only relate to *the statements made by a Member concerning the vote it proposes to give.*'" [italics in original].[1031]

Of course, Macedonia is more than willing to use the Greek leaders' statements against them in court. Such statements are easy to find. The opposition leader in Greece, Andonis Samaras, stated that "Greece has said it favors a name for all uses without an ethnic qualifier as solution to the name row, and put a veto on its NATO and EU accession[...]"[1032] Such statements make it resoundingly clear that "Greece's statements point toward the conclusion that it was the name issue that led to its veto in Bucharest."[1033]

Greece recognizes this and is trying to convince its people that Greece did not veto Macedonia's bid. In actuality, Greece promised to veto, but did not veto, because NATO

[1026] *Macedonians Demand End to Name Negotiations.* http://www.mhrmi.org/news/2010/august19_e.asp . Aug. 19th, 2010.
[1027] *"The former Yugoslav Republic of Macedonia institutes proceedings against Greece for a violation of Article 11 of the Interim Accord of 13 September 1995."* International Court of Justice, Hague, Netherlands. November, 2008.
[1028] *Id.*
[1029] Karavias, Markos and Antonios Tzanakopoulos. *Legality of Veto to NATO Accession: Former Yugoslav Republic of Macedonia Sues Greece before the ICJ.* ASIL Insight. Volume 12, Issue 26. December 2008: 3.
[1030] *Id.*
[1031] *Id.*
[1032] *"Greek PM Pessimistic on Name Solution."* http://macedoniaonline.eu/content/view/17448/2/, Jan. 25, 2011.
[1033] Karavias, Markos and Antonios Tzanakopoulos. *Legality of Veto to NATO Accession: Former Yugoslav Republic of Macedonia Sues Greece before the ICJ.* ASIL Insight. Volume 12, Issue 26. December 2008: 3

countries believed that Greece's threat of a veto rendered it pointless to hold a vote.[1034] Foreign Minister Dimitris Droutsas appealed to Greek politicians' and officials' use of the word 'veto': "I urge you to refrain from using this term in the dispute with [Macedonia]. As much as it sounds patriotic, the use of the word harms our interests in the suit before the Hague-based International Court of Justice," he said.[1035] However, no matter how much political maneuvering Greece utilizes to falsely interpret history, the international community is aware of the truth.

But even if Macedonia wins the case, it would not "ensure that [Macedonia] has a future in NATO and the EU."[1036] This is in part because the ICJ's decision will not have a binding force, and its decision is only advisory in nature.[1037] Greece can "refuse to apply the Court's judgement."[1038] But the ICJ can then "ask the United Nations Security Council to enforce its decision."[1039] However, this is very unlikely.[1040] Still, Macedonia realizes that it cannot let Greece control and manipulate its future, and must continue to protect its rights and interests. That said, even if Macedonia is allowed into NATO and the EU without changing its name, it does not mean that Macedonia and Greece have necessarily settled any of their problems.

[1034] International Crisis Group, *Macedonia's Name: Breaking the Deadlock*, 9 (2009).
[1035] *"Greek PM Pessimistic on Name Solution."* http://macedoniaonline.eu/content/view/17448/2/   Jan. 25, 2011.
[1036] Kosanic, Zoran, *Obstacle's to FYROM's Membership of NATO: A Tougher Agenda Than Expected.* 2009: 6.
[1037] *Id.*
[1038] *Id.*
[1039] *Id.*
[1040] *Id.*

Conclusion

This article has examined the Macedonian-Greek name dispute and negotiation process through many different lenses. Incorporating history, politics and law has been an emphasis in this paper because the dispute is one that is comprised of and influence by all three elements. The dispute cannot be approached – by Macedonia, Greece and the international community – without confronting all of the associated issues described in this paper. Not only will a solution become inevitable, but the stability and peace of the region and Europe may be at risk. However, above all else, the world should unite under one common stance – the identity and existence of a people can never be negotiated.